Front endpaper:
Thomas Bewick
The Wild Bull at Chillingham 1789
Wood Engraving

The Art of Illustration
1750—1900

William Blake. Illustrations to 'The Book of Job'. 1825. Engraving

The
Art of Illustration
1750-1900

R. MARGARET SLYTHE

LONDON   THE LIBRARY ASSOCIATION   1970

First published by The Library Association
7 Ridgmount Street, London, W.C.1E 7AE
1970

SBN: 85365 082 9

Based on a Thesis accepted by The Library Association for Fellowship, 1966

Made and printed in Great Britain by
William Clowes and Sons, Ltd.
London and Beccles

Contents

List of Illustrations

Foreword

ILLUSTRATION is an art of compromise, when the artist is required to work within the confines of a defined context and to allow his drawing or design to be prepared for the accidental fortunes of reproduction. Many artists have been unable or disinclined to master the techniques of illustration; those who have done so continue to search and to experiment in the hope that they may minimise the unpredictable hazards of second-hand impression. With such limiting factors it is remarkable that there should be so many illustrations of sensitivity and beauty.

At the lowest level of book publishing, illustrations may be included merely to bulk an inadequate text. At the highest they may be of such beauty to deserve exquisite bindings for permanent collection. Between these extremes, illustrations may inform and interpret; they may seek to arouse the curiosity of the reader or to entertain. They may provide relief or merely decorative ornament; ideally they should serve as the word illustration suggests, 'to light up' the text.

More often the purpose of illustration is to characterise, especially in books for children. If the camera has informed us and removed from illustration a great deal of information, the best of illustration has defined and animated characters so convincingly that the camera is obliged to re-create that characterisation for it to be acceptable.

If we are to acclaim the art of illustration, it must have a living form. It must insist upon our attention. If it is flat, inert, it will encourage us to turn the page without consideration, to undervalue the book as a whole. The illustrations above all else attract our browsing attention. Ideally the text and illustration should present an even quality with the illustrations in close proximity to the text they complement.

The starting point of 1750 for this survey, written as a thesis for a Fellowship of the Library Association, was determined by the date of publication of some of the most magnificent books in the library of Lord Clark at Saltwood Castle in Kent. The year 1900 was a suitable date to end the survey since by then most illustrations were reproduced by photographic methods; even so it was disappointing to have to exclude those glorious volumes published by Ambroise Vollard, the first in 1900, and many beautiful books published immediately before 1750.

I should like to record my gratitude to Mr. Lynton Lamb, who as thesis assessor contributed much to this survey; to Mr. Reynolds Stone, who owns a fine collection of nineteenth-century illustrated books which he allowed me to use and to discuss with him; and to Lord Clark of Saltwood, whose books feature throughout the survey, who has answered my questions about them over a number of years and who has shown to me his own very exceptional values.

I should like also to thank Mrs. Raymond Lister for lending two photographs and allowing me to reproduce the illustrations by Samuel Palmer and Edward Calvert from her collection; Lord Clark for lending the William Blake 'The Illustrations to the Book of Job' frontispiece; and those who took the photographs for the book, Tony Crompton, S. F. James and the photography staffs of Reading University Library and the British Museum.

1. Book Illustration, 1750–1900: An Introductory Survey

PERHAPS the latter half of the eighteenth century offers illustrations of especial charm because it came immediately before the surge of industrial activity which was to bring about so great a change in all the arts. A period of classical tradition was followed by a romantic revival and with it a new appreciation of the beauty of the natural which swept aside artificiality. This romantic impulse asserted itself in all forms of art and literature. In practical terms, as it concerned book illustration, it meant fewer luxury volumes containing architectural splendours, religious and commemorative works which had filled the libraries of country gentlemen. In their place, books were produced to be read rather than merely to be admired. A reduction in the size of page presented a special challenge to the typographer and the improved quality in both the style and use of type was due largely to three outstanding designers, Fournier in France, Bodoni in Italy and Baskerville in England.

Woodcutting, so popular in the fifteenth and sixteenth centuries, almost disappeared until the latter part of the nineteenth century, when its directness attracted artists of the highest quality, and at the end of the eighteenth century a refined technique of the woodcut was discovered, known as the wood engraving; this was in constant use throughout the nineteenth century and is still unsurpassed. The art of engraving had been mastered by the end of the seventeenth century and throughout the eighteenth century engravers used both the line or copper-engraving and the etching; often they combined the two.

Throughout Europe the printed image was in demand to satisfy a curious public. The need to explain visually promoted the publishing of illustrated books; often a book was illustrated only because it was more likely to sell, but if this was an age of over-illustration, it offers to us today a source of eighteenth-century social scene, of costume, fashion, habit.

There were few new technical developments during the eighteenth century and certainly the influences of the Gothic Revival, of classicism, showed themselves more often in elaborate borders, title-pages and vignettes. In England there was no native baroque art as such, and although there were parallel themes in France and England in the form of topographical books, novels, and poems, there were few books of such luxury in England to compare with those published in France immediately before the Revolution.

Regional and national characteristics formed, in spite of the use of identical materials and techniques, and schools producing tone processes were set up in London, Paris and other European cities.

The mezzotint, used first in 1662 in an English book and soon after for illustrations in books published in Holland and Germany, once again became popular in Europe at the beginning of the nineteenth century. In Italy, the finest artists were illustrating books and reviving an interest in etching. In Spain, Goya was making the first fully effective use of the aquatint and in England, the art of caricature was developing as a symbol of political comment.

In Japan the regional and national characteristic was more marked than anywhere else. The woodcut had been used by generations of oriental schools of art and by 1750 a traditional poetic content had taken over from the earlier romantic theme. Japanese art, expressed in line, pattern and design, differed from Western art, not in materials, but in the concept of painting. Western art allied itself to decoration, story-telling, the portrayal of people and events. In Japan, art was unconcerned with realism; it flowed from the beauty of the painter's skill and the picture he portrayed was an art in its own right. A continuity of styles from masters through apprentices, a use of colour and a wood-block, which produced a print far more akin to the lithograph than to the wood engraving of western artists, together with superb materials and especially fine paper, all combined to produce a unique form of illustration which lasted until the mid-nineteenth century when the mood was spoiled by western influences.

By the end of the eighteenth century book illustration had settled for a standard of dull competence, yet by the first decade of the nineteenth century several of the most dramatic events in the history of book illustration had taken place: Thomas Bewick had rescued the woodcut from oblivion, Alois Senefelder had discovered the process of lithography, the German publisher Ackermann had opened his Repository of the Arts in the Strand, where he produced hand-coloured aquatints from designs of leading artists, and William Blake began the last and greatest of his Prophetic Books.

The nineteenth century was in every way the most formative period in the history of book illustration yet the revolution in all the arts, brought about by a new economic and social system, was responsible for a lowering of standards and a lack of taste unequalled before or since. So much of the illustrative work published was produced as cheaply as possible, the market seemed insatiable for reading matter of all kinds, yet from the many hundreds of books, annuals, almanacs, keepsakes, and magazines, work of any quality was produced by a very few artists, printers and publishers. Often the best artists were employed to work in so narrow a field of experiment that, once a market had been captured, their publishers were unwilling to delimit that scope.

By the 1820's steel engraving, used previously for printing bank notes, was used for the first time for book illustration. There is a quality of brilliance or luminosity unique to this process, and it attracted several outstanding landscape painters, among them Turner and Constable.

Lithography, used with great effect by Daumier in France and Gavarni in Italy, was used with less distinction in England. Rowlandson, who might have made superb lithographs, died in 1827 before lithography publishing became an economic possibility.

By the 1840's, England not only had a railway network but also the steamboat, the electric telegraph and the penny post, all of which combined to accelerate the tempo of living. It was the age of the illustrated magazine when the public demanded visual description of major events at home and abroad. In 1841 'Punch' was published for the first time, a year later the 'Illustrated London News' and, in 1848, Mr. W. H. Smith opened his first railway bookstall. The demand for cheap literature rocketed and the deplorable decline in standards accelerated. It was a dark age for all the arts, yet there remained artists producing high-quality work, more usually those who valued their art more than their income or those who had the means to refuse the demands of insensitive publishers. Comparisons between the original drawings of some of the best artists and the final print which appeared in illustrated magazines give some indication of the misuse and outrage caused by many publishers at that time.

The most effective mid-Victorian contribution to book illustration was the colour print. Much of it was solid, exuberant and tasteless, the typical product of hack publishing, but from the best printers came outstanding work of charm, inventiveness and delicacy. In 1835 George Baxter introduced a process of wood engraving, working in oil colours from as many as twenty blocks at a time, and from this Edmund Evans, one of the greatest colour printers of all time, developed his own colour process. The 1860's was a decade of outstanding coloured wood engravings, gift books and beautiful bindings, a period when illustrative matter was of greater significance than the text. Many of the best illustrations at this time were in books for children, which offered to artists a charming opportunity of fantasy and escapism. The movement of the 60's ended as abruptly as it had begun and it was followed by another decline. Publishers of illustrated journals were demanding even larger blocks together with the mechanical ruling of parallel lines to increase the gauge of tone. Little wonder that artists abandoned all attempts to design; they merely handed wash drawings to the engraver.

The mid-nineteenth century saw a revival too of the illustration in black and white, but in comparison with the earlier author-artist-engraver such as Bewick, the later books, often badly produced and containing works by several artists on the same theme within one volume, were often less than works of art.

In the 1880's the photographic line-block was taking over from the wood engraving and there was a brief revival in the popularity of the deliberately unaccomplished chapbook; both significant symbols of permanent decline in illustrative methods in all but the more expensive books.

The last decade of the nineteenth century was dominated by William Morris and Aubrey Beardsley, strongly contrasting figures; Morris, born out of his time with his love of nature, and Beardsley, very much *fin de siècle*, who cultivated deliberately a mannered artificiality.

Yet, in spite of fashion, the camera and commercialism, at the end of the nineteenth century there remained artists who chose the challenge to their skill demanded by each and all of the autographic methods of reproducing illustrations. Gauguin, from wood carving, rediscovered the living force of the simple woodcut; lithography and all forms of engraving and etching continued to be used. The camera had released the artist from the demands for realism and the artist could once more regard the book illustration as an imaginative art form.

2. Illustration Processes in Use during 1750—1900

THE earliest form of making illustrations, the *woodcut*, had been in use since the end of the fourteenth century and during the fifteenth and sixteenth centuries it had achieved a supreme importance which declined when processes of greater subtlety and delicacy, such as copper-plate engraving and etching, were introduced. At the end of the nineteenth century the powerful and direct force the woodcut can offer was rediscovered and used with great skill and effect by such artists as Valloton, Gauguin, Munch and the Expressionists.

The side grain of a planed plank is used, preferably of pear-wood, but cherry, lime or sycamore are suitable. The design is drawn, traced or pasted on to the wood and sharp knives are used to incise two lines towards one another, forming a V-cut, allowing the wood between to be scooped away. The print is obtained by inking the line cut into that part of the block left raised, after all the non-printing detail has been scooped away from the block; to obtain variations in pressure, the height of the exposed line can be slightly reduced, to soften the impact. The block sometimes appears rough and ill-defined, but many are exquisite. Characteristics of the woodcut print which provide reliable means of identification include evidence of the side grain in the block, and the edge of the impression may show that force may have been necessary to apply ink to paper.

A variant of the woodcut introduced during the fifteenth century provided a perforated or *stippled ground* process. Where the wood had been cut away in the non-printing areas of the woodcut, it was pierced and pricked with an awl-like tool. A graver worked the design on to the side grain of the wood, but this was later replaced by plates of soft metal, usually an alloy of lead, tin and copper.

The *lino-cut* can produce superbly simple and beautiful prints, as Picasso has shown in this century. Lino is easy to cut and where a large flat area is required, either as a printing or non-printing surface, a print can be produced very simply and without the lengthy cutting-away of the woodcut. But the lino-cut lacks the durability and firmness of the woodcut and the crumbling softness of the material causes a tendency to smudge the impression.

The *wood engraving* developed during the nineteenth century as a refinement of the woodcut. A burin, or graver, is used to work upon the end grain of the hard box-wood in an attempt to reproduce the fine strokes and curves of the pen. An incised line, or notch, will become a white non-printing line in a surrounding printing area and a black line to be left standing must be engraved and cleared on each of its sides. Engravers were able to produce the finest lines and the most delicate effects of light and shade; printers used skilful 'make ready', or graded backing, to ensure that areas of solid ink received maximum pressure and the isolated fine lines and edges the lightest pressure possible.

Relief etching was used many centuries ago when limestone slabs were inscribed as gravestones. For printing purposes, a *zinc etching* was introduced. Zinc is very hard, fairly inexpensive and it etches very easily. The design is painted with asphalt varnish on to the polished zinc plate. When the varnish is dry, the plate is immersed in diluted nitric acid. The non-printing areas, that is to say those not painted with asphalt varnish, are etched away. Ink is applied after this first etching, asphalt powder is dusted over those inked parts where further etching is not required and the plate is re-immersed. This process is repeated perhaps six times until the required depth of etching is achieved. The artist may make only the first etch, handing the plate to the process engraver to complete. Half-tones may be achieved by this method, but normally they will be coarser than those produced by the aquatint process.

The autographic processes mentioned so far have been relief or letterpress methods, where the non-printing area is removed from the surface and those parts to be inked and printed remain raised, or for the wood engraving when the graver tool can be used as a drawing instrument and both white and black areas can be left raised at printing surface level.

Other autographic processes are known as intaglio, a method in reverse to the letterpress. Intaglio can be described as recess printing, where the image is incised on to a polished metal plate and filled with ink; the inked surface is wiped clean and the plate is applied to paper with pressure enough to lift the ink from that recess.

In the fifteenth century *copper-plate engraving* had developed from the engraving of plates and goblets by goldsmiths. The precision of the burin can produce delicate, sharply defined lines which taper off to a fine point, distinguishing them from those of an etching.

Steel engraving produces a finer line than copper-plate engraving, but the metal is hard to work, and since the durable qualities of steel can be applied to an engraved copper-plate by electro-plating a steel surface, steel is little used.

One of the most popular processes used from the mid-seventeenth century during the eighteenth and early nineteenth centuries was the *mezzotint*. A copper plate is roughened all over with a rocker, or emery paper can be placed on the plate and passed through a hand-press several times to produce a similar effect. The image is scraped or burnished out of this roughened surface; superb half-tones and shading can be achieved. The mezzotint has a smooth finish and, when magnified, the effect of the rocker tool can be seen.

Copper-plate is used also in the *dry-point* process. Sharp-pointed steel needles, held vertically, incise the metal, producing a burr on either side of the line; this can be recognised as a fine furrow, sometimes it appears white. The ink is held in the roughened or torn edges of the line, causing the printed line to be broader than that in the drawing, and the rapid crushing of the line only allows for very small editions unless the plate has been steel-faced. More usually dry-point is used with another process, often etching, when its powerful style combines well with a more delicate method.

In the early sixteenth century the etching process had developed and for the first time incisions through the drawing were made chemically. Alcohol and whitening are used to remove grease from the polished metal plate; the plate is heated and a ground of wax, pitch, mastic or asphalt is spread thinly over it. The drawing, made with a needle, removes the wax surface; the back and edges of the plate are covered with an asphalt varnish and the plate is then immersed in a solution containing up to ten per cent nitric acid. The plate is examined from time to time and asphalt varnish is applied where further etching is not required. Etched lines are of uniform thickness, with blunted ends; this makes them easily distinguishable from the dry-point or en-graved lines. Earliest etchings were made on iron plates but copper is used most often.

A soft-ground etching can be made to produce lines as if drawn by chalk, by placing a thin sheet of paper on top of the plate and drawing on it with a blunt needle or pencil. Textiles, nets or leathers can be pressed into the soft ground, and graphic artists more concerned with pattern than with fine drawing have derived some imagin-ative results. The soft-ground etching produces results which are inferior to the chalk lithograph.

A similar process to etching but one producing good half-tone on a grained plate is the *aquatint*. Superb effects of shading are possible with a roughened plate if patient control is exercised over the etching process itself. Aquatint is used sometimes in conjunction with line etching.

The scope of the aquatint can be extended by use of the *lift ground* process. Sugar, water and litho-ink are mixed to form the drawing ink, asphalt varnish is applied over the drawing and, when dry, the plate is immersed in water. The sugar dissolves and removes the asphalt surface above it. The exposed metal is given an aquatint grain and etched. In this way the artist can produce single brush strokes or broad pen strokes in the even half-tones of aquatint.

It is possible to *brush etching* fluid on to a plate without the aquatint grain, but the depth achieved by brushing acid is very limited and really dark tones are impossible to achieve.

The *lithograph* is printed from a flat surface, unlike other autographic methods printed in relief or in recess. From its invention at the end of the eighteenth century, the techniques involved in this process, based on the aversion of grease to water, have remained almost unchanged; that is for flat-bed artist's prints on stone, although fundamental changes have occurred in photo-litho processes.

A variety of textures is possible in lithography; the limestone or plate can be grained to give a print resembling a chalk drawing, or it can be polished for use with a pen, brush or knife. The drawing is made with a greasy ink or chalk, and gum arabic is applied to the stone over the drawing. This produces a chemical change in the surface that allows the drawing pigments to be dissolved and exchanged for printing ink. The drawing is normally off-set on to a 'blanket' from which it is printed on to paper, thereby turning the image round as it was originally drawn. Lithography is used with great success in colour work; in the quality of colour tone it is superior to many of the later photographic methods.

3. The Woodcut and the Wood Engraving, 1750–1900

PERHAPS if Thomas Bewick had not been born in 1753, the art of woodcutting might have remained of historical importance only during the time of this survey. Before Bewick, so little use had been made of the wood block during the eighteenth century that only two artists of quality produced work of any prominence: William Hogarth, who made several large original woodcuts, and Jean-Michel Papillon, an engraver of ornamental fleurons and tail-pieces and the author of 'Histoire de la gravure sur bois', an informative book still considered highly today. Choffard thought the work of Papillon beautiful; certainly his blocks are a work of art in themselves, but even so, the fine work of Papillon was more that of an inventive craftsman compared with the artistic completeness of Bewick.

If there are any doubts that Thomas Bewick invented the method of engraving the cross-section of box-wood, that he was the first great exponent of the art is not disputed. In his 'Memoir' he told of his experiments with Dürer prints and the discovery of providing emphasis for the central figure by skilful presswork, in order to achieve superb expression and tone.

Apprenticed in Newcastle, Thomas Bewick walked the twelve miles home to Cherryburn, at first daily and later each week-end, and his knowledge of nature became an intimate, precious thing to him. During his years in London he remained stubbornly provincial and as soon as he felt confidence in his ability, he took his younger brother as his apprentice and set up in partnership with his former master, Ralph Beilby. Again from his 'Memoir' we learn that his 'sole stimulant was the pleasure derived from imitating natural objects'.

The world of Thomas Bewick was not that of a country gentleman. As with Hogarth and Cruikshank, his work reflects the narrow confines of his unworldly experience. Ruskin found this aspect his only flaw or limitation; he considered the work of Bewick to have 'magnificent artistic power, flawless virtue, veracity, tenderness, infinite humour'. When critics of Bewick deemed him untrained, Ruskin corrected this to 'unharmed'. Nevertheless Ruskin's occasional discomfort at the earthiness of some of Bewick's scenes was a measure of the new mood of pre-Victorian prudery, and some designs in subsequent editions were altered to give less offence.

Among his earliest published work were vignettes and tail-pieces, animated scenes often made after he had completed a full day's work. Then in 1790 Bewick published 'A General History of Quadrupeds', an octavo volume containing a wood engraving of every animal known to him. Those animals he could not draw from personal encounter, he took from Buffon's 'Histoire Naturelle'; although these designs are less successful and sometimes even inaccurate, the book has great charm and was immediately popular. Often the animal placed as the central figure is rather flat and lifeless, but the backgrounds are delightful scenes of countryside. The success of the 'Quadrupeds' was followed in 1797 by Bewick's most famous work, 'The History of British Birds', published in two volumes, the first, 'Land Birds', in 1797, and in 1804 'Water Birds'. Many of the published copies were hand-coloured. The birds are very real, superbly plumed, their temperaments skilfully shown in their eyes. Often Bewick placed a bird on a rock to give especial prominence to its feet. To the naturalist, the engravings are superior to those in 'Quadrupeds'; to the art historian they are a forerunner of the Romantic movement with a truer sense of balance between central figure and background, offering a greater opportunity for Bewick to develop foliage and natural features within that unique oval he liked to use. John Piper has said that Bewick's great gift was 'unclouded vision' applied to the block itself rather than to the design. Perhaps Bewick visualised his designs as ovals, composing an oval block completely as a picture, disregarding the more usual approach of drawing a design first on paper. Certainly the curvilinear of the oval and the soft beauty of the background offset the flat, accurate, often unanimated characterisation of his creatures.

However, no such inertia appears in his lively vignettes or tailpieces, nor in the wood engraving Bewick considered his best work, 'The Wild Bull at Chillingham'. Made in 1789, while producing designs for 'Quadrupeds', the bull was one of a herd of wild cattle and Bewick was obliged to stalk the animal in the park at Chillingham. The Bull is magnificent, powerful to an extraordinary degree, one forefoot anticipating attack, the tail raised in apprehension. The foliage on the trees is exquisite and the bull treads upon a world of beauty among the grass.

In 1818 he illustrated the 'Aesop Fables', but although many of the designs are beautiful, Bewick found restricting the need for association with a text.

His last work, 'Memoir', written just before his death in 1828, was not illustrated yet it provides great insight into the man and his work. The first half of the book deals simply with his early life, the latter half is somewhat pompous and moralistic. We discover his tastes and his habits: his admiration for Scott, his disgust with Byron and the pleasures of his evening jaunts to the public house with his dog, Cheviot.

Thomas Bewick.
Vignette.
Wood engraving

Many artists who followed Bewick must have envied him the completeness of his art, his ability to design, engrave, print, experiment with press-work and print again. Excessive pressure used to emphasise the central characters of his blocks caused the text of his books to appear over-black and woolly, but Bewick cared little for typography. His innovations revolutionised the art of wood engraving and his pupils, including such fine engravers as Robert Johnson, William Harvey, Charlton Nesbit and Luke Clennell, were the first of many artists to use his methods.

Only a dozen or so artists were using the wood engraving as a medium for book illustration at the time of Bewick, among them William Blake. It would be difficult to find two more dissimilar artists so closely contemporary. Bewick popularised the art of the wood engraving with sharp, detailed, accurate designs, perfect miniatures of nature. The work of Blake had nothing to do with natural objects: abstract ideas flowed from him, making his designs dark, evocative, full of mystery and movement, far closer to the twentieth century in feeling. Blake claimed that he was inspired by visions and most histories of art call him without question a visionary. However, Kenneth Clark is prepared to accept that the only genuine 'moments of vision' that came to Blake he portrayed in the illustrations to Thornton's 'Pastorals' and a few other minor works; most of Blake's visions were inspired by his intense visual memory of works of art by Michelangelo, Tibaldi, Gothic effigies, even Babylonian reliefs.

In 1821 Blake experimented with wood engraving and made seventeen blocks for another of Thornton's works, Virgil's 'Eclogues'. These designs are rather fine, with strong, ecstatic little figures, enormous suns and moons often setting upon or rising between hills; sometimes lonely or menacing expressions, always very much alive.

Although he tried every known method of book illustration, William Blake remained outside any pattern of development. His impact is far greater today than during his lifetime although he did have a few contemporary disciples, including Edward Calvert and Samuel Palmer. Palmer made only one wood engraving, of a primitive cottage surrounded by harvest reapers with tree clumps and a sickle moon,

Edward Calvert.
The Brook.
Wood engraving

a beautiful design. Both this engraving and some of Palmer's etchings show strongly the influence of Blake. Edward Calvert made seven wood engravings, dramatic, sentimental, full of moving forms with little feeling for perspective and scale, with Blake's same disregard for line or finish; his early work is very beautiful, in particular 'The Chamber Idyll'. In more recent times, the mood of Blake has infected the work of many modern artists, among them Graham Sutherland, whose tree and thorn forms take startlingly similar shapes.

Blake's art was expressive of English Romanticism, but the complicated presentation of visual memory, combined with imagination and a determination to convince that his philosophy was a thing of mysticism, isolated him from all others. Certainly his method of expression was unique; not since Dürer had the wood block been so alive and the inter-relationship between characters and dark and shade so remarkable.

It would be misleading to convey that between 1750 and 1828, when Bewick died, a year after Blake, there were no other artists making use of the woodcut and wood engraving for illustration purposes. Hogarth, better known for his engravings, and Papillon, for his decorative use of the wood block, have been mentioned already and both artists are included elsewhere in this survey. In addition, many books published during that period contained borders, ornament and initial letters cut from wood; but the laborious method of plank cutting resulted in prints which lacked precision and of clumsy proportion. The genius of Dürer, three centuries earlier, so important in the development of Bewick as an artist, was creative at a time when competitive publishing was unknown; Bewick's innovations offered an economic alternative to lithography. Not only was the improved method far quicker to print, since the letter-press wood block and the text can be printed together, but the block can be given as much expression as the copper plate, a quality which endeared it to many artists who found suspect the comparative ease of lithographic reproduction.

It is in the white parts of the wood engraving that light and life occur. An over-darkened design is often the mark of a fussy, unoriginal, unassured artist, one who does not know where design stops and ornament begins. Nineteenth-century artists who submitted designs for publishing with little regard for the advantages or short-comings of the method of reproduction have been replaced in later editions by artists with a greater awareness of the significance and sensitivity of text with visual accompaniment.

Most early-nineteenth-century artists experimented with the possibilities of both the lithograph and the wood engraving. Those artists who achieved successful wood engravings must have welcomed the composition roller patented by George Baxter and Robert Harrild in 1835, which was capable of producing a superb tone range, using as many as twenty oil colours. Baxter used his roller to print the vignettes in the two-volumed 'Feathered Tribes of the British Islands', by Mudie, in 1834 and two years later for the illustrations to Mudie's 'The Heavens' and his own 'Agricultural and Horticultural Gleaner'. Most of the eighty-seven book illustrations printed by Baxter were frontispieces; many of the scenes he depicted were of royal occasions: the Coronation of Queen Victoria, Opening of Parliament, Royal christenings, although more usually these were published as single prints. Another book containing illustrations printed by Baxter in 1846 was Isaac Frost's 'Two Systems of Anatomy'.

By the 1840's wood engraving in England had established itself so firmly that it was influencing artists in Europe and a new movement was asserting itself. Many histories of illustration call the 1840's a decade of monochrome, due in no small measure to the appearance of illustrated magazines, such as 'Punch' and the 'Illustrated London

News'. For the first time the reading and book-buying public had become an economic factor in publishing. With the new and extensive use of original wood engravings in both books and magazines, publishers confined their interests to drawings in black and white to keep costs to a minimum. Large numbers of books for children were published during the 1840's, many of them in weekly parts, such as the series 'Gammer Gurton's Story Books', which sold at sixpence each or ninepence with a coloured illustration. 'Home Treasury Toys' was another with a surprisingly high standard of reproduced illustrations by such artists as Dürer, Holbein, Raphael and rarely less than a Royal Academician.

Many books published with lithographs, engravings and etchings continued to incorporate woodcuts and wood engravings for ornamental decoration, but fewer books of encyclopedic content, on birds, animals, fish, astronomy and botany, illustrated solely by wood engravings, were published during the mid-nineteenth century; those that were achieved an unbelievably beautiful effect of colour tone.

The art of satired humour was developing and artists such as George Cruikshank, John Leech and Charles Keene were contributing to the journal 'Comic Almanac', so brilliantly illustrated that any twentieth-century counterpart seems commonplace. Perhaps the personality of Cruikshank most accurately assessed the character of mid-nineteenth century illustration although his best illustrations are etchings. Charles Keene, one of the finest artist-draughtsmen, produced a great many superb illustrations for 'Punch' and it seems extraordinary that publishers did not persuade him to illustrate books.

By the 1850's almost all books were published with some illustrations, almost always wood engravings or lithographs. The emphasis had shifted dramatically by now from collector to reader, and books were smaller, easier to handle and included more text than at any time previously. Far too many of the books published in the middle of the nineteenth century were deplorable by any standards, but it is perhaps unfair to condemn more than a century later what must then have been little less than a social revolution to early Victorians. It was in 1851 that Langton discovered how to photograph drawings on to wood, but the process was not in general use for another twenty years and then only for work of the most ephemeral nature; it was a further twenty years before it was used consistently for book illustration.

Curiously, technical accomplishment in book production at this time gave far greater prominence to engraver, printer and publisher rather than to the artist. Presumably the artist's ability to illustrate was not in doubt and the satisfactory printing of his work was still somewhat of a novelty. Perhaps the most significant skill was that of the trade-engraver, who engraved the artist's design for him. The Dalziel brothers were trade-engravers first and publishers afterwards.

George and Edward Dalziel set up their Camden Press in 1857, and most of the illustrated books published in England between 1857 and 1875 seem to bear their imprint. One of their first publications, Allingham's 'Small Book of Verse, The Music Master', contained eight engravings by Arthur Hughes, one by Rossetti and one by Millais. In the preface, Allingham thanks 'those excellent painters who on my behalf have submitted their genius to the risks of wood engraving!'

Perhaps the best known publication printed from the Dalziel Press was 'Poems by Alfred Tennyson, Poet Laureate, illustrated by T. Creswick, J. E. Millais, W. Mulready, C. Rossetti, D. McClise, Clarkson Stanfield and J. C. Horsley', published by Edward Moxon in 1857. Some poems have head-pieces by one artist and tail-pieces by another, an extraordinary mixture of old and new. The four Rossetti illustrations make the Moxon edition especially memorable, although Tennyson found these designs offensive and they created enormous problems for the printer. Millais illustrated the text with the greater accuracy; Tennyson thought the Millais illustrations ideally suited to his poems, yet they convey little personality, impact or emotion. Trollope also found pleasing the illustrative work of Sir John Millais; Millais illustrated his novels 'Orley Farm' and 'Framley Parsonage', but there is not one outstanding illustration in either book.

At this time the Dalziel brothers introduced a series with coloured illustrations which they called the 'Dalziel Fine Art Gift Books'. Millais produced illustrations for 'Parables of Our Lord' in 1863. The engravings are rather fine but the typography is over-fussy and pretentious and the era of the 'red rules' had arrived, when the page was framed by a rectangle of narrow red lines printed around both the text and illustration. Presumably the ruled lines were intended to give an appearance of uniformity throughout the book, at a time when several artists with differing styles were contributing to the same text. Sadly the lines succeeded only in creating an insipid, dated, faded look which lessened the impact of the colour illustrations.

A most skilful and professional artist of the nineteenth century who produced designs for Dalziel was Arthur Boyd Houghton. His drawings have an unusually large amount of white in them, giving them a directness, a focal compactness. With Tenniel, Millais, Pinwell and others, Houghton contributed to Dalziel's edition of 'Arabian Nights'; the translation of this was as poor as the paper it was printed upon and the rather splendid designs were surrounded by oppressive, unnecessary borders. Houghton contributed illustrations too to the 'Round of Days'. Perhaps his best known designs were those engraved by Dalziel for 'Don Quixote' in 1866.

One of the earliest uses of colour printing for illustration was in 1857 by Charles Bennett for the 'Aesop Fables'. Edward Lear, a most able colour illustrator of ornithological subjects, was more often associated with the lithograph at this time, but his 'Book of Nonsense' in 1846 was an important milestone in the study of book illustration. In the first edition of the 'Book of Nonsense' the designs were reproduced lithographically, but subsequent editions had the same designs printed as wood engravings. But the significance of Lear was less concerned with artistic or technical achievement than with content. The balance of illustration and text, and the obvious humour in both, had widespread effect and from that time entertainment became a prime factor in publishing, particularly in books for children.

Arthur Boyd Houghton. 'Don Quixote'. 1866. Wood engraving

There was an old man who said, "Hush! I perceive a young bird in this bush! When they said — "Is it small?" — He replied, "Not at all! It is four times as big as the bush!"

Edward Lear. 'Book of Nonsense'. 1846. Wood engraving

The brothers Dalziel were publishing much of the best work of the period, although even their most successful books had a marked imbalance between text and illustration. The techniques of printing coloured illustrations seem to have been mastered and the colour tone throughout the many hundreds of books published at this time is a very remarkable achievement. The Routledge series 'Dalziel's Fine Art Gift Books' all contain very beautiful pictures, even if many of them are hardly illustrative. Among the most pleasing are Birket Foster's 'Pictures of the English Landscape', published in 1862; 'Home Thoughts and Home Scenes' in 1865; 'Wayside Posies' in 1867; and 'A Round of Days' in 1866. Miscellanies seem best suited to the almost scrap-book effect of combining the work of several artists in one volume and 'A Round of Days' is a rather nice example. The illustrations, by a variety of eminent artists, depict original poems by some of the most celebrated poets of the day. Many of the illustrations are of sea or water scenes; the faces are directly appealing, with fear or sentiment, the mood so right for peaceful Victorian contemplation.

Embellishments for the lithographically illuminated gift books at this time were often wood engravings, as in Henry Shaw's 'New Testament', published in 1865, and 'Two Centuries of Song', in 1867. Henry Noel Humphreys was another of the great printers of colour lithography who chose wood engraving for some of his work, including 'River Gardens' in 1857, 'Ocean Gardens' in the same year, and in 1858 for

'The Butterfly Vivarium', printed in two colours and subsequently hand coloured. Joseph Cundall's anthology in 1848, 'Songs, Madrigals and Sonnets', contained seventy pages, sixty-two of them with colourful wood engravings, mostly border embellishments.

E. J. Sullivan has said that 'the art of the sixties has been the most British, even the most English expression yet found since Hogarth'. Forrest Reid saw the 1860's as a movement; Gray saw it as one which failed to bring art to the masses when Pre-Raphaelite artists of quality, Rossetti, Millais, Hughes, became bored with the technical difficulties of the wood engraving and returned to the freedom of paint. The Dalziel brothers managed to persuade superb work from these painters, unlike Routledge, Moxon and other contemporary publishers, who lacked imagination as directors.

It is difficult to understand how a decade of such superb illustration could have been associated with so little feeling for typography. David Bland has said that the 1860's was a time of many fine wood engravings in exceedingly ugly books. It could not have been simply a case of publishing at the lowest possible price; if so, the illustrations would have been as deplorable as the pallid texts. Vivid, gilded bindings must have made impressive Victorian room decoration. The Sunday book preoccupation of familial Victorians, with their fondness for group activity, demanded an emphasis of illustrative content; the text was illustrative of the visual image more often than the reverse, and it seems probable that the typography seemed quite adequate until photographic methods of reproducing illustrations diminished their impact within the book as a whole.

Ruari McLean considers the book-making of Edmund Evans superior to that of the Dalziel brothers. Evans was perhaps the most successful engraver and colour printer of the generation. His colours, superbly mixed, were as bright and clear as any achieved by Baxter. Evans' better known works include Chevreul's 'The Law of Contrast and Colour' in 1860; 'The Art Album' published by W. Kent in 1861; 'The Psalms of David' published by Sampson Low in 1862; and 'A Chronicle of England BC 55–AD 1485', written and illustrated by James Doyle, with four hundred and seventy pages of colour printing at its best, the colours as fresh as if they had just been painted, the typography clear and beautiful, with precise margin notes to précis the text.

Evans was a lifelong friend of Birket Foster and together they produced some very fine work. In 1859 they published 'The Poems of Oliver Goldsmith', with ten prints

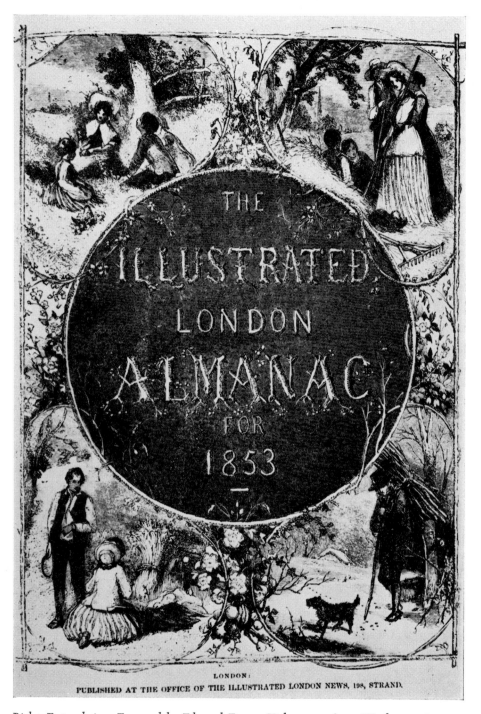

Birket Foster design. Engraved by Edmund Evans. Title page. 1853. Wood engraving

which looked more like paintings than illustrations, and in 1860 Thomas Miller's 'Common Wayside Flowers'. The work of Birket Foster includes much of the subject matter so attractive to Bewick—soft countryside, thatched cottages, elms, church towers, stiles, sheep, and above all a peaceful prettiness instantly recognisable. Blues and greens predominate, any rare use of red becomes a focal point. Birket Foster's wood engravings were printed also by the Dalziel brothers, who in 1859 printed some Birket Foster illustrations for a collection of 'Odes and Sonnets'; these designs were rather unusual, more illuminations than illustrations.

A successful and prolific contemporary of Birket Foster was John Gilbert. His illustrations had a feeling of activity, often of violence. He was primarily an historical painter and his book designs made no concessions to the engraver. Between 1856 and 1858 he made a great many superb illustrations to Shakespeare plays, and he was a frequent contributor to 'Punch' and the 'Illustrated London News'. The illustrations of John Gilbert are all rather fine and very much alike and this is a significant problem in searching for exceptional quality among mid-nineteenth-century book illustration. Hundreds of books, many of them beautifully illustrated, with insignificant typography; jolly, often beautiful bindings and a certain heaviness in the stitching and make-up. An overwhelming similarity dulls any endeavour to assert superiority.

Another printer of fine colour work, again with very indifferent typography, was Benjamin Fawcett. His interest lay in the world of the naturalist and he produced, over a period of more than thirty years, books on a series of authoritative, almost encyclopaedic topics. Many of these were issued in monthly parts and subsequently bound. In 1849 Fawcett collaborated with the Rev. Morris on a 'History of British Birds' and 'Nests and Eggs of British Birds', both containing wood engravings, partly colour-printed and partly hand-coloured afterwards. Fawcett used A. F. Lydon as an illustrator for thirty years and this contributes to the feeling that the volumes are part of a set, which they were not intended to be. In 1879 Fawcett published the two-volumed 'British Freshwater Fishes', by William Houghton; the sixty-four coloured wood engravings are so fresh, one might think that the fish had been freshly caught and laid upon the page; in addition there are a great many zoological diagrams and landscape vignettes within the text. Other major publications by Fawcett included in 1882 'The Ruined Abbeys of Great Britain' in two volumes, and between 1860 and 1880 'A Series of Picturesque views of seats of the Noblemen and Gentlemen of Great Britain', the text by Morris, all of the illustrations by A. F. Lydon; quite the most gigantic project attempted by Fawcett, who sold more than ten thousand copies.

These enormous volumes are grand in the Victorian manner, of technical achievement rather than artistic originality; nevertheless superior examples of Sunday books, frequently sought by present-day book collectors.

Henry Vizetelly was a publisher best known for his colour lithography for Humphreys and Jones. Wood engravings he printed included a festive anthology in 1851, 'Christmas with the Poets'; in 1853 'Uncle Tom's Cabin' and again in 1853, Martin Tupper's 'Proverbial Philosophy', which included illustrations by Gilbert, Tenniel and Foster. Vizetelly was later fined, imprisoned and ruined for his published translations of the works of Zola.

At this time hardly any artist of note seems to have declined to draw illustrations for magazines. Charles Dickens edited a periodical 'Once a Week' from 1859, in which much of his own work was serialised and illustrated; and 'Punch' and the 'Illustrated London News' were both filled with social satire reflected by the finest artists of the day. Perhaps in retrospect the 'Punch' of today will seem to have symbolised as successfully the contemporary mood, but it seems unlikely. Undoubtedly the camera is largely responsible. Editors must define visually in the most economical and acceptable form as it seems to them at the time.

Of all mid-nineteenth-century artists perhaps the work of Sir John Tenniel is best known by generations of children. His illustrations in 1865 to Lewis Carroll's 'Alice's Adventures in Wonderland' must have found their way into every literate home during the past century. The story was originally entitled 'Alice's Adventures Underground' and Lewis Carroll had himself drawn the illustrations to the first edition —rather spiky, unfeeling drawings which did little to endear the characters to the reader. Carroll's disapproval of Tenniel's drawings is one of the better known literary feuds of rivalry between author and artist, and in their combat of mutual disapproval and counter suggestion, most bystanders must surely sympathise with Tenniel. Even allowing for the displeasure of the Rev. Dodgson, or Lewis Carroll, at his publisher's insistence that another artist should be engaged for the subsequent edition, it seems churlish and short-sighted of Carroll not to have been charmed and delighted with Tenniel's visual conception of Alice and her friends. Forrest Reid saw Tenniel as a humorist with a flair for drawing animals; maybe, but Alice is drawn with simplicity and an economy of line and from that drawing emerges a warm, alive Victorian child, sometimes self-assured, often very much the reverse, within an environment far beyond the imagination of most and presenting a superlative to even the world of Mary Poppins in twentieth-century nurseries. In 1871 the Alice sequel,

*Sir John Tenniel.
'Alice's Adventures in
Wonderland'.
1865.
Wood engraving*

'Through the Looking Glass', was published, assured of success by the established imagery of author and artist. The only other really successful book illustrations Tenniel drew were for the 'Ingoldsby Legends' in 1864. Cruikshank and Leech also contributed to this volume; all three managed to convey a good deal of humour visually. Where Tenniel found little scope for humour he became over-sentimental, as in the sixty-nine drawings he made for Thomas Moore's 'Lalla Rookh' in 1861. Tenniel made some steel engravings too, for Brook's 'The Gordian Knot'; these differ little from his wood engravings, but are in no way exceptional. Tenniel was an outstanding illustrator of 'Punch' and in 1901 a collection of these illustrations was published in book form.

Some of the most enchanting children's book illustrations ever drawn were those by Richard Doyle for 'In Fairyland', printed by Evans and published by Routledge and Warne in 1870. One especially unforgettable illustration is a twelve-inch strip entitled 'Dressing the Baby Elves', predominantly a soft green, with fierce little faces on enchanting bodies, bedevilled by mischief. This appealing magic accelerated the rapid growth in children's book publishing.

Kate Greenaway.
'The English
Spelling Book'.
1885.
Wood engraving

One of Edmund Evans' protégées was Kate Greenaway, one of few illustrators to achieve substantial financial rewards during her lifetime, whose name designates the annual Library Association accolade for the best illustrator of children's books. Her earliest work was illustrated with lithographs but once Edmund Evans became interested in her work, she conformed to his preference for the wood-engraving. Her illustrations to the books of other authors were less successful but her first book of verses and drawings, 'Under the Window', published by Evans in 1877, sold 20,000 copies on publication. Her later work seems insipid by comparison; the skill of Evans' printing must have contributed to the bolder appearance of the earlier work.

Richard Doyle. Tailpiece from 'The Princess Nobody'. 1884. Wood engraving

3

Kate Greenaway, Walter Crane and Randolph Caldecott were among illustrators of the series of Toy Books published in such vast numbers by Evans.

Another highly successful illustrator of children's books was Arthur Hughes. He had a remarkable sympathy with his authors, and his work exuded that sentimentality so beloved by Victorians. Often the figures in his drawings appear too large, giving a cramped effect; certainly he appeared to prefer to work within a confined space. He illustrated 'Tom Brown's Schooldays' in 1869; in 1871 George Macdonald's 'At the Back of the North Wind', which had appeared first in serial form in the 'sixties; and in 1872 Christina Rossetti's 'Book of Musical Rhymes, Sing-Song', one of the most popular of all Victorian nursery books. Each page has a poem and an uncoloured illustration—a beautiful composition of sympathetic shapes, often without background.

During the 1880's Joseph Crawhall published from his Leadenhall Press a flood of cheap, jolly comic books, and throughout Europe there was a brief revival of the chapbook, peddled from manufacturing centres such as Newcastle and Chartres. These books contained old ballads and stories, and in spite of their clumsy format often included very pretty designs, hand-coloured predominantly with reds, yellows, greens; influenced strongly by medieval manuscripts and by William Blake. One of the most popular, 'His Wallet Booke', a collection of angling poems by Isaac Walton, is filled with cows, sheep, beetles, anglers and flowers; quaint, homely and often witty.

One of the most distinguished wood engravers of the latter part of the nineteenth century was William James Linton, who published three books on the history and practice of engraving—solemn, rather scholarly discourses on art and beauty as seen through Victorian eyes.

By the end of the century, paintings and wash drawings were photographed upon sensitized wood-block; far too often engravers were too much concerned with colour, too little with line or form, and artists were angered by the published prints. An exhibition of original wood engravings was held in London in 1895, to which Charles Ricketts, Charles Shannon, Reginald Savage and Lucien Pissaro contributed; to eliminate confusion with illustrations reproduced photographically, their designs resembled pen drawings that might have been printed far more easily by the process they sought to condemn. Ricketts and Shannon collaborated to edit an occasional periodical, 'The Dial'. Limited to two hundred copies, it included original woodcuts and lithographs. Today it seems stilted with enormous margins surrounding ornate designs—very *fin de siècle* in feeling.

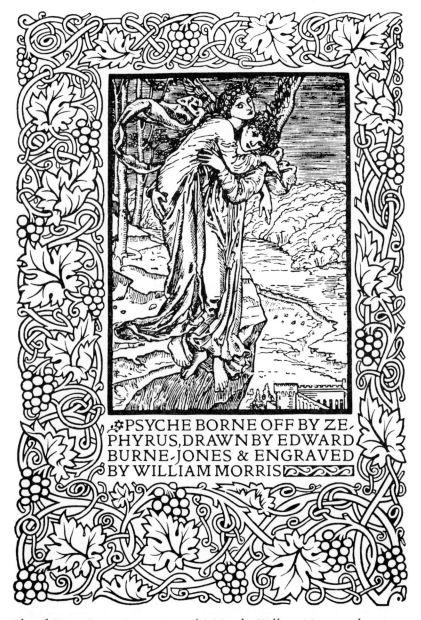

Edward Burne-Jones. Frontispiece to 'A Note by William Morris on his aims in founding the Kelmscott Press'. Engraved by William Morris. 1895. Wood engraving

The greatest figure of the transition period between original nineteenth-century and modern illustration was undoubtedly William Morris. With Aubrey Beardsley, who drew almost exclusively for photographic reproduction, Morris dominated the last decade. Like Bewick, Morris began by copying Dürer woodcuts and in 1865 he made some engravings of designs by Burne-Jones for an edition of the poem 'The Earthly Paradise', but it was never published; Morris returned to this poem in 1890, engraving the title-page which was used for the first edition only, as the block was destroyed subsequently by fire. Morris had a love for the medieval and a conviction that books could be beautiful in a totally self-contained way, as many other forms of artistic expression, such as a piece of beautiful architecture within ugly confines could never be. His book-making was superior in every aspect and it may be claimed that modern fine standards of printing and publishing owe much to those of Morris. With Walter Crane, who designed many attractive woodcuts and engravings, Morris founded the Kelmscott Press, yet few of the books from their press have outstanding illustrations; they employed far too many inferior or mediocre artists.

Morris thought himself a decorator rather than an illustrator. Surprisingly, it was the lank and anaemic style of Burne-Jones he chose most often to decorate; their collaboration produced rich, elaborate, massed exaggeration of quite simple themes. Together they represented symbolic beauty, Victorian prudery in direct contrast to the often gross themes of Beardsley. Morris engraved other Burne-Jones drawings for 'Pygmalion and Image', 'The Ring given to Venus', and 'Tännhauser'; all were discontinued before publication. The 1896 Kelmscott Press edition of Chaucer is rather fine, with Burne-Jones designs decorated by Morris, presented in a beautiful gothic folio with a two-columned page, surrounded by deep borders of floral designs and intricate initials. Another outstanding example of their association was the 'Socialist Romance' of Morris, sometimes entitled 'A Dream of John Ball'.

In the concessions they made to Morris the decorator, Kelmscott Press books mirrored the solid tastes of Victorian ornament. With Beardsley, Morris rebuked utilitarianism; each with a liberated sense of design established an appreciation for extravagance and above all technical skill. Peter Mey speaking of the ornament of the 'Book of Kells' has said, 'In times and regions that possess a fully developed figurative art, ornament plays the part of accompaniment only, but there are also eras in which it assumes the full value of great art, because the needs of contemporary expression are limited to the domain of ornament.' Perhaps the transitional period at the end of the nineteenth century was such an era.

In Paris the 'Almanach des Artistes' of 1776 listed only five wood-cutters and engravers, and three of those were letterers. Among them, Jean-Michel Papillon, author of 'Histoire de la gravure sur bois' already mentioned, one of a family of accomplished engravers, may be considered an exceptional artist. Choffard greatly admired the work of this inventive craftsman, who designed vignettes, fleurons, head- and tail-pieces, all symmetrical patterns of exquisite precision. However, nothing in his designs suggests he might have made outstanding original use of the innovations by Bewick had he lived long enough to do so.

Enthusiasm for the new wood engraving techniques came to France from England at the beginning of the nineteenth century, but it was not until the 1830's that the ornamental use of the woodcut in books illustrated by copper engravings gave way to wood engraving as the sole illustrative method.

Early nineteenth-century books with woodcut ornament include an edition of 'Fables' of La Fontaine in 1802. Illustrations to the works of La Fontaine would make a study in themselves; no other author can claim so many illustrators. One of the first books in France with wood engravings was the 'Fables', illustrated by Devéria in 1826. In 1839 Johannot, Adam and several others illustrated another edition, skilfully, but with unappealing animal characterisation. Undoubtedly the most dramatic of the dozens of illustrated 'Fables' was that which included engravings of Gustave Doré in 1868. It is a splendid quarto volume with restrained typography and vignettes which look almost etched. The main designs, however, are over-large Baroque exaggerations of melodrama, with little animal sympathy.

Between 1813 and 1825 Alexandre Desenne made several woodcuts, mainly vignettes, for the Hermite series of de Jouy. Desenne had a freer style and a less rigid approach to even the most formal work. In many ways, Desenne bridged the eras between ornamentation and the revival of the wood engraving.

As in England, European journals from the 1830's were illustrated both with lithographs and wood engravings. In France, 'La Caricature', 'Le Charivari' and 'Le Monde Illustré' presented superb contemporary political and social satire, mirrored by the finest artists of the day. French journals with a kind of cheap prettiness were more frivolous in appearance than their English counterparts.

Honoré Daumier, one of the great artists of nineteenth-century illustration, is considered in some detail with lithography. However, Daumier designed more than one thousand wood engravings for journals and it seems strange that he was not persuaded into book illustration. His positive, direct humour and sympathy might have made a

37

considerable impact; Cervantes' 'Don Quixote', for instance, might have been better illustrated by Daumier than by Doré.

Inevitably the novelty and crisp precision of the wood engraving caused its excessive use, especially of the vignette, no longer presented as restrained head- and tail-pieces but set throughout the text. One early over-enthusiast was Tony Johannot; his designs for the 'Magasin Pittoresque' of 1833, both wood engravings and lithographs, made any text appear irrelevant detail. In 1839 Johannot made eighteen full-page woodcuts and ninety woodcuts throughout the text for Abbé Antoine-François Prévost's 'Histoire de Manon Lescaut et du Chevalier des Grieux', one of the great French romantic novels, a very beautiful quarto volume with China paper printed on one side only for some of the first edition copies. Johannot's illustrative interpretation is faithful both to the characters and to the mood of eighteenth-century France.

By now artists and publishers were commuting freely between England and other European countries. The 'Gil Blas' of Lesage in 1835 had ruled borders, unmistakable evidence of English influence. Gigoux produced six hundred wood engravings for 'Gil Blas', so bulky that it was published in parts, and, by public demand, later parts had even more illustrations and less text.

The two-volumed Petrus Borel translation of 'Robinson Crusoe' of 1836, including two hundred and fifty wood engravings by Devéria, Boulanger and Nanteuil, seems now to be an extremely tasteless presentation. The pictures are fairly simple and pleasing enough, but they are overpowered by elaborate borders which totally extinguish their impact; indeed the picture is often hard to find.

Often considered to be the most outstanding book to be published in France at this time, 'Paul et Virginie', by Curmer, included the designs of many engravers. The text includes an index to these artists; many of them are English. The typography is well above average, but the text is too frequently broken by illustration and in 'La Chaumier Indienne' only a single phrase separates each picture. The full-page illustration was out of favour; in the manner of William Blake, designs and text were often fully integrated. It is as pointless to say that such excessive illustration is irritating to the reader as it would be to condemn the comic of today for the same reason. To the book buyer in France at that time the text was merely the pretext for a sequence of pictures.

The most original and exciting illustrator of the mid-nineteenth century was Grandville. So many of his contemporaries produced lifeless illustrations to the works of La Fontaine that the Grandville designs of 1839 are a pleasant surprise. At last an artist extracted humour with imagination and mystery from the animal world of La Fontaine. In 1840 Grandville illustrated 'Robinson Crusoe' and in 1842 'Scènes de la Vie Privée et Publique des Animaux', both with delightful and strange designs. In 1844 he made some illustrations for 'Un Autre Monde', an exotic book in every aspect, and in 1847, for 'Les Fleurs Aimées', in which the designs are so very pretty that the humour Grandville gave to them is rather diminished. His illustrations in 1848 for 'Don Quixote', including some steel engravings, are unexceptional.

Colour wood engraving, so popular in England, achieved little favour in other countries; the surprising decade of the 1860's seems to have flourished unenvied by Europe. Perhaps the mood was too English, like subtle humour which is rarely international.

Some European artists, however, were working in London. One of them was Paul Gavarni. In London he produced two-colour wood engravings in a striking style; often he gave more detailed treatment to the focal point in his design. Gavarni worked in London and in Paris and one of the most splendid illustrated books of the nineteenth century is the two-volumed 'Le Diable à Paris: Paris et les Parisiens', published in Paris in 1845 and 1846. The first edition, printed on one side only of China paper, has a frontispiece and two hundred and eleven full-page caricatures by Gavarni, together with eight hundred woodcuts in the text by Bertall and others. The wit of Gavarni, displayed with a piercingly critical eye, makes this a brilliant book in every way.

Gustave Doré, often called the 'last of the Romantics', dominated the years 1850 to 1880, which might otherwise have been rather a void in France in terms of wood engraving. Doré produced thousands of designs for journals, particularly for 'Le Monde Illustré'; he liked to work on a large scale, from black to white, and even the smallest of his drawings appears larger, in spite of an excessive mass of detail. Doré seemed often to lack confidence to decide when his design was complete and he continued far too long, yet his style was unique, dramatic and instantly recognisable, which contributed in no small part to his considerable fame during his working life. All of his work appears well printed; much of that of his contemporaries less so. The scale of Doré must have been welcome relief after so long and excessive use of the vignette.

Art historians deplore the popularity of Doré while artists of greater ability were ignored. One of the sorrows of scholarship is to see a non-too-well-informed public grasp at something, albeit inferior, obvious in impact, overtly offered. Many feel such scorn of Doré unfair; few artists have produced designs more menacing or more sinister, and the black depths of his work depict an air of fantasy with considerable skill. In 1855 Doré illustrated the 'Contes Drolatiques' of Balzac with small sinister drawings almost buried in the text. His illustrations for Dante's 'Inferno' between 1861 and 1866 were published at his own expense and, like those in 1863 for 'Don Quixote', resemble paintings and have a fantasy relationship with the text. The canvasses painted by Doré were huge and confused; they found little recognition in Paris. However, his 'Bible' of 1866, with an illustration on every four to eight pages, established his acclaim and encouraged him to try religious themes for his painting. By now he merely handed wash drawings to engravers for his book illustrations. Among his later work, he made some steel engravings for 'Idylls of the King' in 1868 and 1869 and some rather lurid wood engravings for Jerrold's 'London' in 1872.

Auguste Lepère, who made both wood engravings and later original woodcuts, made a significant contribution to book-making in France after photographic methods had taken over most of the mechanics of reproducing illustrations. He was one of a group of enthusiasts for the original woodcutting revival who formed in 1897 the 'Société des graveurs sur Bois'. Through its journal, 'L'Image', it presented all that was best and worth preserving in the art of designing the wood block and formed transitionally a starting-point for a new generation of artists. A typical issue of 'L'Image' included line engravings by Lucien Pissaro, free plank woodcuts by Auguste Lepère, who was joint-editor with Tony Beltrand, and rather impressive canvas tone-studies after Eugène Carrière.

Henri Rivière, at the end of the century, was imitating the shapes and mood of Japanese artists with rather pleasing colour-washed designs. As Desenne had bridged the eighteenth and nineteenth centuries, now Felix Valloton was the most obvious link between styles of a century later. The era of characterisation was giving way to motives of free expression, in positive, direct shapes, without excess of detail.

If Paul Gauguin had not gone to Tahiti, he might never have been attracted to the woodcut as a means of expressing that world which became so much of his life. His earliest wood block he cut in 1894, with lines made with fine needles between deeply gouged ones, producing a mixture of subtlety and violence so characteristic in all his work. Often the pressing of his block to paper or canvas was uneven, and subsequent colour blocks may not have covered completely; the results are individual, original and strangely restful, a kind of welcome abdication of the over-precise.

Affection for the wood engraving spread to Germany too. The Menzel illustrations to 'History of Frederick the Great' must be included in any survey. Adolph Menzel, a contemporary and rival of Doré and a superior artist in every way, experimented with all of the illustrative methods at some time. His wood engravings for historical books are unbelievably detailed, in a way that makes one feel he must have been there, at each scene himself; the portrayal of human suffering, mental anguish and dignity has never been depicted more movingly by any artist.

Other illustrated nineteenth-century books of especial interest include 'Another Dance of Death', published in 1848, with six satirical wood engravings by Alfred Rethel, now no longer hostile as they might then have seemed; folk songs and fairy tales sentimentally illustrated by Ludwig Richter; pious little period-pieces of German life; and the jolly comic-strip type illustrative work of Wilhelm Busch. Two characters evolved by Busch, Max and Moritz, became endearing mouthpieces of social satire in German journals.

Doubtless books illustrated by wood engravings were published between 1750 and 1900 in other European countries, but the impetus came from London or Paris. Few Italian artists seem to have been attracted towards the wood engraving other than for ornamentation. An Italian history of music which may be considered typical of many luxurious eighteenth-century publications, 'Storia della musica', by Giambattista Martini, published in three volumes between 1757 and 1781, is very much a collector's prize. Voluptuous copper engravings form the main illustration but borders, vignettes, initials in profusion ornament every page, and most of these are wood engravings. The text is considered authoritative still today and, significantly, Italian artists, while as prone to excessive illustration as those elsewhere, seem to have contributed illustration to a text with the assumption that the text was the prime function of the book. No doubt this may be due in some part to an abundance of folio publishing in Italy; artists who were unwilling to associate with a text could publish prints of their designs in this way.

Wood engraving reached America as soon as a copy of one of Thomas Bewick's books had crossed the Atlantic, and immediately artists began to make imitative copies of his work. One of the first competent wood engravers in America, Alexander Anderson, made copies of many imported wood-engraved books, including a version of Bewick's 'Quadrupeds' published in America in 1802.

Felix Darley was one of the more original illustrators who tried a number of techniques and, even though he was influenced strongly by both Doré and Cruikshank, his wood engravings of the two Irving books, 'The Irving Sketchbook' in 1848 and 'Irving's Knickerbocker's History of New York', published in 1850, are alive and rather fine. In 1866 Darley produced two-tone wood blocks to illustrate 'A Selection of War Lyrics'.

W. J. Linton, author of 'A History of Wood Engraving in America', considered the 'American Drawing Book of 1847' to be 'perfect' even though the wood-engraved illustrations were contributed by many artists and had little uniformity about their presentation. Linton himself produced a number of pleasing wood engravings after drawings. He was firmly against experiment and innovation and he criticised loudly Timothy Cole, who redrew photographs into line drawings and translated those drawings into wood. Cole produced superb colour tone in his wood engraving and was the first American illustrator to discover original techniques.

Another fine experimental engraver was Howard Pyle, who wrote and illustrated several of his own books, including 'The Book of Pirates', which was very eighteenth-century in feeling, and 'The Wonder Clock' in 1880, illustrated with Dürer-like wood engravings, the text and illustration united by ruled lines and decorative initials.

By the 1850's illustrated magazines were occupying most of the competent American illustrators. Every town aspired to have its own local periodical and the profuse illustrations printed in them were reproduced by both wood and copper engravings. A number of them are mentioned in this survey with the engraving.

It was not until after the mid-nineteenth century that American artists began to develop a national style, until the Baxter colour era in England and the 1860's, which had no counterpart in America, created a void and an incentive. Before that time all American illustrators seemed influenced by Dürer, Hogarth, Bewick and Doré, and even towards the end of the nineteenth century European artists with strong individual styles, such as that of Aubrey Beardsley, influenced all kinds of graphic art in America.

Few American illustrators deserve mention beside the great illustrative artists in Europe, but in a developing country, where visual media was often the only method of comprehensible communication, the part played by illustration in the social life of Americans cannot be overstated. The engravings in the first edition of 1852 of Harriet Beecher Stowe's 'Uncle Tom's Cabin' did more to excite public indignation and awareness of the need for slavery reform than did any of the more conventional political media. The greatest contribution to the art of illustration in America during the eighteenth and nineteenth centuries was to inform and to attract attention, and the ephemeral nature of most of the illustrations produced seems an irrelevance when considered within their own context.

From the unoriginal, competent visual history of America, the remarkable unique art of the woodcuts from Japan seems especially delightful. Japanese artists produced an art so incompatible with western art that even where the materials and purpose are identical, comparisons are quite impossible. Pictorial means of expression both may be; there any similarity ends. Japanese painting has always been more limited in range than European, but within those limits, more perfect.

Hiroshige. Oi. c.1840. Wood engraving

The art of the Ukiyo-ye, of the colour-print artists, primarily a style of painting, was first introduced in mid-seventeenth century by Matahei, and it was continued by all major schools. Moronobu, who drew small compact figures, may have made the first book illustrations and plates issued as broadsheets, and from him a oneness of style developed which, through fine artists such as Okumura, Masanobu, Harunoba and Kiyonaga, was followed faithfully by apprenticed pupils. Often the similarity of styles and the lack of facial expression makes final identification of the artist difficult. Many of the most well-known masters have specific and individual characteristics in their work; it would be impossible to confuse, for instance, the small-featured demure faces of Harunoba with the rounder, placid ones of Shunsho.

Before the mid-eighteenth century the wood block had been hand-coloured after printing, but from the 1740's blocks were normally printed in soft reds and greens; the prints became smaller, the figures more slender—changes no doubt due to the artists' unerring sense of balance and a desire to limit the impact of the use of colour. Some twenty years later additional colours were used, always with the same dignified tone. One of the outstanding users of the *beni-ye*, the two-colour print, was Masanobu; his characters, usually female, were queenly juno-esque forms, sweet, graceful and exquisitely dressed. His scenes were idyllic with curving rivers, the cone of Fuji beyond rice fields, the corner of a tea-house beside bamboo.

In 1764 Harunoba introduced the *nishiki-ye*, the brocade print, in many colours, and there followed a period of enormous output by superb artists, among them Masanobu, Shunsho, Yeishi, Utamaro, Hokusai and their pupils and followers. Harunoba (also spelled Harunobu) prints were almost always of flower-like, fragile women; his themes were hardly unique but his style had an individuality and an enviable quality that makes western women feel extraordinarily clumsy.

The colour print of eighteenth-century Japan was the most skilful collaboration between publisher, designer, engraver and printer. The mulberry-bark paper they used must be added as a vital contribution: it ensured a bloom and radiance not achieved anywhere else in the world. The artist supplied his drawing on transparent paper and indicated colours required in printing. The engraver pasted the drawing face down onto a block of hard wood such as cherry, in the manner of Dürer rather than Bewick; the lines were left in high relief and for each colour a separate block was made; nothing differed from the western technique so far—if anything, the Japanese blocks were rough and unfinished by comparison. A little size made from rice was used to give a firm consistency to the colours. Colours until the nineteenth century were of vegetable origin and there is now an imbalance in those early colour prints where the greens, yellows and browns have remained fairly constant and the blues and reds have faded. In a letter from Hokusai to his publisher, the artist suggested a maximum printing of two hundred copies before the block might wear beyond reasonable use.

By the eighteenth century the Kabuki Theatre was an amusement for the lower classes, and theatrical subjects were frequently chosen by book illustrators. Both in the finest books published for the Samurai and in the more humble versions for the Yedo folk, by now very much more literate, artists seem to have been obsessed by a

Isoda Koryúsai.
At the Well.
c. 1772

Toni Kiyonaga.
Mother and Servant with
Child beneath a Willow
Tree.
c. 1782

Wood engravings

45

love for the gayer and more frivolous aspects of life. Dozens of colour-print books appeared entitled 'Pleasures of Yedo', depicting gallants escorting courtesans and geishas on their way to tea-houses or theatres; pleasure boats on the Sumida river or of beautiful gardens with flowering shrubs and trees. Interiors often depicted a single lady idling away the day with pets and yo-yo. A rather superior publication of 1776, 'A Mirror of Beauties of the Green-houses', was filled with illustrations of courtesans by Shigemasa and Shunsho. Shunsho was perhaps the greatest master of theatrical design. Only male actors were permitted to perform and his work often depicts skilful female impersonation. Another significant theatrical designer was Sharaku, a Nō dancer, who produced a number of prints of theatrical scenes in 1794, intense and disturbing expressions of characterisation.

By the end of the eighteenth century a political undercurrent within Japan disturbed the nature and purpose of the colour print and there followed almost a *fin de siècle* and a sophistication quite unknown before in Japanese art. But such involvement did not destroy the pure landscape art that existed in Japan long before it came to European painting. Birds and flowers were familiar themes too, and of the landscape artists the finest were Utamaro, who in 1790 was making prints of pure landscape, totally featureless, merely shapes and colours of delightful designs; Hokusai, with an audacious bright use of colour; and Hiroshige, softer, gentler, the closest of all Japanese artists at that time to western art. Of those artists involved with scenes of strife and turbulence, the work of Kuniyoshi is most striking and he presented an unusual appreciation for pageantry during the mid-nineteenth century.

The art of the Ukiyo-ye artists was ultimately one of design. Laurence Binyon considered 'as pure design, this body of work is unrivalled in any other country, except perhaps by Greek vases'.

There is life, not accuracy, in their drawing; the arrangements are artificial but they form inventive pattern. Today they seem less original than they must have done to mid-nineteenth century European artists, who learned from them to break from the dogma of realism and to use human form and landscape feature as elements of pictorial pattern. Degas, Manet, Van Gogh, Toulouse-Lautrec and Beardsley certainly show influences of Japanese art in their work.

Once oil-painting reached Japan the colour print was dead; this occurred during the 1860's. Engravers there retained their skill, but Japanese artists had destroyed their native genius by allowing Western influences to affect their purpose. Subsequently their drawing is merely pretty or dramatic.

'The Insect Book', illustrated by Utamaro in 1778, contained a sophisticated soft use of greens and white, occasionally other colours, a very alluring combination. In 1791 Utamaro illustrated 'Bird Book', a collection of humorous songs with a scientific diagrammatic form of drawings. Utamaro books were splendidly produced, superbly printed, with an extensive use of metallic gold and silver. Between 1817 and 1849 Hokusai made audacious vivid illustrations for the fifteen-volumed 'Mangwa'.

The last important artist, or Ukiyo-ye artist, Kyosi Gwaden, illustrated in a number of different styles 'A History of Japanese Art' in 1884; and in 1894 an edition of 'Fables' of La Fontaine was illustrated with strong, violent designs by the 'best artists of Tokyo'.

These illustrated Japanese books published during the eighteenth and nineteenth centuries and quoted often as superior examples of bookmaking are extremely rare outside Japan and national museums. But copies of prints of this exquisite, unique art found their way to Europe and to America, and the art of illustration, not only the wood block, was and remains today deeply affected by them.

4. The Etching, 1750–1900

WE are told as students that the pure etching has no burr; that any burr softens the line, which proves it cannot be an etching; that the lines of the printed engraving have shallow entrance and exit points where the burin has marked the design on to the copper plate, whereas the lines of the etching are blunt-ended as the acid will have bitten evenly through the design drawn on to the ground. But such characteristics can be simulated and artists have experimented continually to achieve a unique quality by disregarding such rules. The French artist Jacques Callot, a contemporary of Rembrandt, invented a special etching needle sharpened on one side like a knife; this will give a tapered end to a line if it is turned in the fingers. Also, it is not impossible to end a line abruptly with a burin and, by spinning an ordinary etching needle between the fingers, a line can be tapered. In addition to these sophistications, the degree to which the inked line is wiped can provide other variations.

The practice of etching the design and subsequently engraving the plate has always been a popular one. More often than not, the artist made the etching which he then handed to a trade engraver to complete.

Theóphile Gauthier, in the preface to the first issue of the 'Journal of the Société des Aquafortistes' in 1862, considered that a 'successful etcher requires a decision, a sureness of touch, a capacity for recognising the final result'. Not every art historian has held the etcher's art in such high favour. Ruskin considered the art of etching too accidental; that it was impossible to shade delicately, to imitate nature, to etch a cloud, a head of hair. He considered engraving to be a superior discipline and engraving he considered 'the art of scratch'. Sir Hubert von Herkomer, Slade Professor at Oxford during the 1890's, considered that etching needed to be accompanied by some other tone process, by aquatint, dry point or engraved retouches; the artist Turner preferred mezzotint to be used with the etching to provide greater depth of emotion. Certainly the pure etching demands from the artist a visual imagination quite unlike any other illustrative method; this is lessened by the re-examining of prints between states, nevertheless one must assume that many etchings, even very successful ones, have turned out quite unlike the artist's original intention.

It is doubtful that any artist using the etching method during the century and a half

1750–1900 was not consciously influenced by the technique and genius of Rembrandt. As Dürer had been the model for the expressive qualities of the woodcut, so Rembrandt became the inspirational source for etchers. Many artists made imitative copies of his etchings and even where their results were unsuccessful, they added something to the significant place that the etching has always had in Rembrandt's art. Perhaps no other illustrative method provided so diverse an aim or purpose or was so vulnerable to the fortunes of fashion, but in times of favour etchings by the finest artists were bound into volumes, many of them exquisite; a title-page and index were often the only pretentions to book-making, yet where the art is great enough any text would seem intolerable distraction. Finest of all such magnificent volumes are those containing the etchings of the mid-eighteenth-century painters, Canaletto, Tiepolo and Piranesi.

Even though the thirty-one Canaletto views of Venice were made between 1740 and 1743, they were reprinted continually for many years. Some of the views are authentic, others are imagined and these are freer, livelier; consistently Canaletto achieved a shimmering brilliance, an extraordinary clarity and an intimate activity quite impossible to produce in paint. The quality of his visual composition is such that elements of his designs seem to be stage-set, as though he had drawn a backcloth and manœuvred his pieces of perfect architecture into place. It seems that a bright beam of light has passed along his scenes; sometimes this gives his work almost an impressionist feeling. His work is accurate without being overprecise and the characters which animate his views provide a natural realism to the scene.

It is hardly surprising that the crisp clarity of Canaletto's etching should have encouraged many artists to attempt similar views. It is a measure of his skill how many of them failed; instead they produced faded, dramatic, clumsy, artificially posed compositions.

Gianfrancesco Costa produced two volumes of Venetian views between 1747–56, one hundred and seventy plates in all, a set of tourist documentation, lacking in almost all of the qualities one admires in Canaletto, whose influence is even more clearly apparent upon the etching of his nephew, Bernard Bellotto. Eight of his thirty-seven plates are exactly imitative of Canaletto's style.

The illustrative work of Giovanni Battista Tiepolo was limited to two series of etchings. The first set, 'Capricci', was published by Zanetti in 1749, and the second. 'Scherzi di Fantasia', in 1775. The 'Capricci' series have a linking theme in that they are all of groups of women, children and soldiers. There is an uncertainty, a sinister mystery, even sorcery about the atmosphere of all of the etchings and the characters are drawn so beautifully, with imagination, economy of line and rhythm. Tiepolo leads himself to the vision of death, the absorbing theme of the 'Scherzi' series. Most of his etchings are of out-of-doors themes of indeterminate purpose, with additional elements on the ground such as trophies and shields; but in the later series he has added macabre skulls, bones and tortured serpents. The mystery and witchcraft have become menacing and evil; the etchings have a disquieting compulsion.

Magic had a prominence in eighteenth-century Italy, even in its intellectual life; no artist conveyed it better than Tiepolo. His strokes rarely crossed, the effect was fluid and free; often his faces were strikingly beautiful, none more so than the young woman with her arm resting on an enormous urn (Plate 6, Capricci). Almost all of his designs include animals, usually a dog, sometimes a monkey. Even the most macabre of his themes is drawn with delicacy and etched with lightness; his compositions are graceful, elegant and bathed in exquisite light.

Giambattista Piranesi etched the fourteen plates for his 'Carceri' in 1745; published by Bouchard, in this first version the etchings were light, every stroke was revealed. The darker version which Piranesi worked later, Bouchard published in 1761; this is the series most often seen. Many well-known figures of art and literature recorded their approval of the darkened version, among them Coleridge, De Quincey, Turner and Gauthier.

Prison scenes were used often as theatrical decor in eighteenth-century Italy and were not uncommonly depicted by artists; Marot and Bibiena used them as themes for their work. The massive fury of Piranesi was never bettered; man is defeated merely by witnessing the enormity of his fortress. Piranesi lights his scenes of the 'Carceri' as a stage director might set a tragedy; brilliant shafts of light remind those inside that life goes on outside; the shadowed depths express all the despairing loneliness and futility of spirit. Piranesi used a blunt needle to remove the ground; he never marked the copper plate. He achieved immense height with long, uninterrupted lines; his foreground strokes were strong, slightly undulating. The expansive freedom of his work must have stunned admirers of Canaletto and Tiepolo.

Piranesi etched some thirteen hundred plates, most of them after 1750, showing the splendours of the Ruins of Rome; all of them of dignified architecture, softened by humbler backgrounds, buildings and brambles, bushes, foliage, composed with a supreme skill into poetic masterpieces. The publisher Guiseppe Wagner encouraged Piranesi to produce his prodigious social commentary of eighteenth-century Italy and

Giambattista Piranesi. Prison Scene from 'Carceri'. 1761 (darkened version). Etching

the status of Wincklemann in Germany was enough to create an insatiable demand.

The 'Vedute di Roma' are bound into massive volumes, each containing etchings on a few related themes. Fifty-nine etchings are included in 'Vedute di Roma; Basilica di St. Paolo, Street Markets, Del Ponte Molle'; many of the etchings have footnotes of explanation, they are the most magnificent documentary of all social activity: soldiers, workmen, noblemen, ladies, boats and bridges. Another set bound in 1764, 'Antichita d'Albano di Castel Gandolfo', provides an informative textbook and a pleasing combination of architectural detail and beauty. The double frontispiece is exquisite and no architectural aspect is missing, even pavings and wall stones are included. It is interesting to note that after 1770 Piranesi etched clouds in his sky; none had appeared before that date. The great art of Piranesi was personal and grand in the Venetian manner.

The influence of Piranesi was immediate and extensive in all branches of painting, decoration and architecture. In England, Robert Adam used Piranesi's plates for a book by the brothers Adam on architecture and interior design; Adam's designs showed a marked debt to the drawing of Piranesi. Robert Adam brought several Italian artists to England, among them Piroli, one of Piranesi's pupils; Piroli, in association with Flaxman, illustrated Homer, Hesiod, Aeschylus and Dante. And in 1798 Piranesi's sons were summoned to Paris to establish a school of engraving, ensuring his influence to be even greater during the nineteenth century than in his own lifetime.

Curiously, this outstanding use of the etching was not continued in Italy and certainly it was unmatched elsewhere. Luxury book-making was at its most superb in France, but even the greatest art from the finest European painters in the most exquisite bindings remained incomparable to the bound, almost accidental volumes of etchings of Piranesi.

In fact, eighteenth-century books containing etchings are difficult to find; the engraving was more often used. One of the most splendid is the two-volumed 'Prints for Drawings' with notes by Charles Rogers, published by John Bondell in 1778. The illustrations, soft-ground etchings, are imitative of existing drawings; Charles Rogers has added critical and biographical notes. Volume one is exquisite; the plates are followed by copious notes of mythology and other themes, interspersed with very beautiful vignettes. Corrections and additions complete this scholarly, informative volume. The historical bibliography in volume two is a remarkable piece of scholarship; no detail is omitted. Dedicated to the sovereign, it serves as a magnificent, luxurious representative of the eighteenth century, in total contrast to the era of democratic commentary and criticism which followed.

In England William Hogarth was staging a revolution, albeit an unconscious one, among the illustrative arts. His engravings of satires and political caricature were being published in enormous subscription issues; his art, while not aesthetically remarkable, symbolised all the discontent and ridicule of Establishment. It is surprising to discover that he died in 1764, before the moral indignation he expressed so vividly had gained impetus. Certainly, able artists throughout Europe considered his blatant and often vicious mockery a refreshing breeze through eighteenth-century superficiality. With Hogarth the new mood of public dissent had become a visual theme.

The caricature introduced by Hogarth was perfected by two abler English artists, Rowlandson and Gillray. Thomas Rowlandson is best known for his superb use of aquatint; 'The Smugglers', 'The Excise Men' are exceptionally fine examples, powerful, economically drawn, the designs filled with life and character. But Rowlandson did make a few pure etchings; sadly, they were badly devalued by an appalling application of colour within his outline. Two popular etchings, 'Farriers' Shop' and 'Easter Monday', show what a superb eye he had for the ridiculous. He was an extravagant dissipant and much of his work depicted the coarse, the brutal. His work has great range: he drew landscape, seascape, architecture, sport, town and country life, almost always satirised. Much of his work was published by Ackermann and a good deal of it was sold in Europe. We are told the young Delacroix was feverish with excitement when he first saw Rowlandson's work; synonymous with accelerating discontent in France, it must have seemed a gigantic breakthrough to be seen to characterise malcontent so openly.

Rowlandson etched forty plates which were published separately and also in a bound version in 1816 entitled 'World in Miniature'. He made many contributions to journals too, but he did no book illustration. Quite the best of his humour is shown in 'Christie's Auction Rooms'; the longer one looks the more one finds to amuse. 'Ducking a Scold' is another popular burlesque Rowlandson made of country life; all his work is superb social commentary.

James Gillray, a favourite of George III, was best known for his wild frolics of hunting scenes or burlesques of tradition. Many of his five hundred etchings and engravings are of the French Revolution or associated themes. The caricature remained a solely English art with the obvious brilliant exception of Daumier in the nineteenth century; no eighteenth-century French artist was able to maintain so well-aimed an attack as that of Gillray, whose wrath lashed out at political establishment and sovereignty more in the caustic manner of Hogarth; Rowlandson had a more tolerant humour.

James Laver has said that Rowlandson was a painter who engraved and Gillray a draughtsman who etched. Gillray assessed the English royal family and Napoleon Bonaparte more skilfully than any artist or literary figure. He used the captioned comment drawn into his design in the cartoon manner of today. Some of his drawings were macabre in the extreme; it would be difficult to imagine a more ghoulish scene than 'Un petit souper à la Parisienne'. The best work of Gillray was done between 1787–95; vitriolic comment had less significance after the Revolution, when the print-buying public demanded a more peaceful, optimistic content and landscape painters were encouraged to make etchings.

James Gillray.
Old Wisdom.
1780.
Etching

54

Paul Sandby was another English artist whose first prints were aquatints, but his etchings were more accomplished. His etching of 'John Balfour's Coffee House at Edinburgh' in 1758 is particularly fine, as were many of his country scenes, especially 'English Pastoral'. His work had a directness, a vigour, an underplayed humour and his human groups, especially those which include children, are sympathetic studies; his feathery trees are unusual and pleasing. Sandby's work, like that of Bewick, was not well printed.

Thomas Gainsborough liked to combine aquatint with etching. His pure etchings are meticulous but tame, he found irksome the etching needle. But his soft-ground etchings and aquatint such as 'Gypsy Encampment' are soft, charming compositions; they were published in 1797, after his death, by Boydell.

The 'Anatomy of THE Horse' by George Stubbs, published in 1766 and measuring 22 inches × 17 $\frac{1}{2}$ inches, was in every way a unique and historic publication, invaluable still to animal painters. Stubbs prepared his drawings for these fine etchings from dissected horses; the intense accuracy of his work is remarkable. Stubbs, with his anatomical method of presentation, was a style innovator quite as important as Hogarth, Gainsborough and William Blake.

The middle years of William Blake were taken up with the production of two major works in relief etching: in 1804 he published 'Jerusalem' and in 1808 'Milton'; he printed, published and sold his own work, supervising progress throughout.

His first published work in relief etching was in 1789, 'Songs of Innocence and Experience'; some of the copies were hand coloured. Blake would have considered it absurd to separate text and illustration, and in his engraved work he engraved the text too, directly on to the plate. In 'Songs of Innocence' the verse flows into the figures; children, angels, prophets and even God are distorted into a combined design.

Only two of Blake's etched works were made in the conventional intaglio method; these were 'Ahania' and 'The Book of Los'; neither is outstanding.

In 1793 he published a relief-etched poem 'America—a Prophecy' and a year later 'The Book of Urizen', aquatinted and hand-coloured.

William Blake was a beholder of past and future, less a mystic or a visionary than a seer. He believed that men who do not live in the freedom of spiritual illumination sink into the oppression of animal life.

His poem 'Jerusalem' was described by Gray as 'the grandest effort for imaginative art in England and in every way the biggest of the beautiful books'. Only one version of this, the longest poem ever published, is known to exist in colour; Mrs.

Blake or some other colourist must have found it a formidable consignment. Turning over the pages of 'Jerusalem' is like confrontation with some tremendous force, moving figures strive on every page; not surprisingly, the impact is lessened by overpowering energy.

The 'Milton' illustrations, published four years after 'Jerusalem', are rather fine, but again there is an overwhelming sameness about the pages; certainly the text of the Milton is submerged by the Blake designs. His unique art is felt most forcefully when one turns from his work to that of any other artist. His incredible flamboyance makes other etchings appear commonplace initially, but soon one is relieved to find delicacy, understated aestheticism. Like any excess, a little goes far.

In 1804 the Water Colour Society was founded and many of its founder members made etchings. None of the artists seems to have achieved fame, but many of their pleasing compositions have reached National Print Rooms. An artist well represented at the British Museum is Robert Hills, who made rather original, pleasing animal and landscape etchings.

A highly individual artist who lived only twenty-seven years was Girtin; like Gillray and Rowlandson, he rebuked prettiness, yet his twenty soft-ground etchings for 'Picturesque Views of Paris' are superb, full of character and insight. Several editions of bound copies of this set were published.

A friend and contemporary of Girtin, Joseph Mallord William Turner, one of the great English landscape painters, used etching with mezzotint for a number of his plates and combined etching with dry point or aquatint for his 'Liber Studiorum', issued as a series of plates between 1807–19 to illustrate the potential of landscape composition. Turner expected to make one hundred plates to the set, but completed only seventy-one—the project seems to have been too prolonged to sustain his interest. Those he did complete are masterpieces of organic line; in the hands of the great artist such a line becomes the definition of the beholder's vision, one fills in, completing each composition quite naturally. Turner colour-washed ten of the designs. Many of them have a bleak, lonely, wild feeling; always the shapes are superb.

John Constable collaborated with the mezzotinter David Lucas and together they issued several sets of landscape studies. Constable made three original etchings for his 'Milford Bridge near Salisbury'; they are filled with light and air, very original in texture and atmosphere.

In addition to Turner and Constable, undoubtedly the two greatest artists in England, a wide circle of their contemporary artists made pleasing etchings. Crome,

Daniell, and Read all made line etchings; Cotman and J. R. Cozens made soft-ground etchings; and Alexander Cozens, Prout and David Cox made aquatints. It is important to remember that as a theme, landscape was a refreshing novelty at the beginning of the nineteenth century; now many of these etchings seem over-familiar, entirely unextraordinary and with little impact.

Many of these artists were members of what is known as the 'Norwich School'. John Crome, often known as 'Old Crome', made several etchings for his own pleasure; they were not published until after his death. J. S. Cotman published a 'Liber Studiorum' too, often to be found in shabby condition in bookshops, and many line etchings. His first set in 1811, on 'Howden Church, Yorkshire', is particularly fine. In 1814 he made twenty-seven soft-ground etchings bound into a volume entitled 'A narrative of the Great Festival of Yarmouth on Tuesday 18th. April 1814'. In 1816 and 1818 he published two books on the architecture of Norfolk, careful, loving pieces of admiration. In 1819 he produced a book on the 'Sepulchral Brasses of Norfolk and Suffolk' and in 1822 two folio volumes containing one hundred plates of the 'Architectural Antiquities of Normandy'. Cotman had an architectural feeling for historic buildings; art historians have always rather scorned his work. Obviously he was influenced by Piranesi, but he wisely avoided the melodrama which Piranesi achieved with such personal triumph.

Henry Cave made forty-one plates which were bound into a volume in 1813, 'Picturesque Buildings in York'. The etching of Cotman overshadowed that of other members of the Norwich School, but the best architectural etchings of John Coney came closest to him in quality. In 1832 Coney published 'Ancient Cathedrals, Hôtels de Ville and other Public Buildings in France, Germany and Italy' with thirty-two plates and a brief descriptive text in French and English. The plates average 20 inches × 16 inches; they are concerned with Gothic architecture in organic line, boldly etched but not especially well printed.

The publisher Ackermann was at the height of his output of luxury volumes, illustrated almost always by aquatint, intended for the libraries of country gentlemen. Almost all of his prints were issued in parts initially, usually by subscription and later beautifully bound. His 'Microcosm of London' issued between 1808 and 1810 is typical of his work. Priced at seven shillings per issue, each included four colour plates. J. C. Nattes 'A Tour of Oxford' was issued in twenty-five parts in 1805 at twelve shillings each; a fascinating documentary, beautifully produced. Nowhere in the world was better publishing available. Other outstanding aquatints published by Ackermann were J. E. Smith's 'A Tour to Hafod' in 1810 and Thornton's 'Temple of Flora' in 1797–1807; this included mezzotints as well as aquatints.

Samuel Prout's 'Rural Cottages in the West of England' in 1816, and a series of 'Rural Cottages in the North of England' in 1821, two unpretentious and charming series of prints, offer as significant a social commentary as any history book. And between 1814 and 1825 William Daniell made twenty very beautiful aquatints and several etchings combined with aquatint to illustrate 'Voyage round Great Britain', published in eight volumes; they are like mammoth story picture books, detailed and totally absorbing.

Bonington (included in greater detail with Lithography) made only one etching in

Thomas Shotter Boys.
Église Sainte-Eustache.
1833.
Soft-ground Etching

58

1826, 'View of Bologna'; the foreground buildings have strong uncrossed lines and, as in his lithographs, the background of tower and church fade beyond.

Thomas Shotter Boys made few etchings; they are little known. His first etching was in 1823, of a copy of a vase belonging to Baron Denon. The soft-ground etching he made in 1833, so evocative of Canterbury, has no shading and looks rather unfinished. Around the same time he made an aquatint with soft-ground etching of the 'Corner of the Palais de Justice'; it is rather feebly drawn with too little shading. The British Museum has this drawing on tracing paper, which Boys seems to have transferred to the metal plate. Also in the British Museum are drawings for soft-ground etchings of 'Église Sainte-Eustache' and 'Views of Paris with the Pantheon and the Towers of Notre Dame'; both have marvellous roof shapes, a beautifully perspected skyline and rather more foreground than Boys normally used; they are certainly the finest etchings he made and are closer in emotion to his lithographs. Between 1851 and 1853 Boys made some etchings and lithographs for Ruskin's 'Stones of Venice', of little consequence artistically, but they seem to have pleased Ruskin, who wrote, 'copies from my pen drawings etched by Mr. Boys with a fidelity for which I sincerely thank him.' The last known etchings of Boys were made after Ruskin's drawn copies of Turner for Ruskin's 'Modern Painters', Vol. 4, in 1856; one of them is to be seen at the Victoria and Albert Museum. Boys was a superb draughtsman and this is a skill shown to full advantage in the etching. The 'Connoisseur' of May 1921 called him 'a Great London Delineator'. Most of his best work is in the Bibliothèque Nationale in Paris.

Much of the best etching of the early nineteenth century was printed by the trade engraver Thomas Stothard, who died in 1834. Hardly a literary classic was printed without illustration and the most prolific writers of the day, Fielding, Sterne and Smollett, provided constant occupation for engravers; the lithograph and the wood engraving had not yet established themselves as commercial illustrative processes.

In 1841 an Etching Club was formed in London. Retrospectively it seems the only outstanding members were Haden, Palmer and Millais, but its aim was to encourage a growing enthusiasm among collectors of the etching. For a period of perhaps thirty years of the nineteenth century, the etching was the first choice of those who considered themselves to have taste in print collecting; after that the etching became a neglected art in England, though less so in France; now it is little more than a music-hall joke. Etchings once printed in large numbers can be purchased now for a few shillings and those of the finest artists were printed in such limited numbers that invariably they find their way into National Print Rooms.

But in 1841 the Etching Club issued its first Annual with optimism; as one might expect, the landscape etchings are rather fine, the portraiture undistinguished and the issue as a whole almost idyllic, prettily styled, nothing more. The first publication of the Club, also in 1841, 'The Deserted Village' of Oliver Goldsmith, included forty plates and seventy-nine small etchings, dainty and charming. Joseph Cundall acted as publisher for the Club; later he became a photographic publisher. Two of his best known publications for the Etching Club were Gray's 'Elegy' in 1847 and Milton's 'L'Allegro' in 1849. The text printed by Whittingham is on very thin paper; the etchings on the same paper have been pasted on to heavy card. Another edition of Milton's 'L'Allegro' and 'Il Penseroso' was published in 1855 with twenty-four large steel etchings by Birket Foster, better known for his wood engravings. The Milton poems are printed in red and combined effectively with delicate steel etchings.

Sir Seymour Haden, a well-known surgeon, made two hundred etchings, professional and vigorous, and showing the influence of both Rembrandt and Haden's brother-in-law, James Whistler. Haden, a founder member of the Etching Club, seems to have etched only three plates for the Club. Mostly his themes were of landscape; and he was a keen fisherman, which led him to etch five rather fine angling scenes; Wales was another of his favoured scenes. His designs are filled always with trees.

Richard Doyle, an artist responsible for many magical wood engravings, achieved immortality as an etcher for his cover to 'Punch' in 1849. He also made some very fine etchings in 1851 for Ruskin's 'The King of the Golden River'. An author whose work seems to have received continual illustration by a variety of able artists was Oliver Goldsmith. The best of his work to be illustrated with etchings seems to have been 'The Poetical Works of Oliver Goldsmith' published by Charles Griffin in 1866. The etchings are by several artists but the effect is nevertheless very pleasing; the typography is undistinguished but at this time illustrative content was of much higher quality than the printed text.

Samuel Palmer made eight plates for the Etching Club. Palmer was greatly influenced by the work of William Blake. His style was minutely detailed, very meticulous in the Victorian manner; he made thirteen etchings in all. In 1855 he etched a plate with two designs on it for 'Songs and Ballads of Shakespeare' and in 1861 he etched one large plate 'The Herdsman'. After Palmer's death, his son published in 1883 his designs for Virgil's 'Eclogues' and in 1888 those for Milton's 'Minor Poems'. Both these included some illustrations photographically reproduced.

Samuel Palmer. The Bellman. 1879. Etching

61

The 'Eclogues' etchings are perhaps the best of Palmer's work. He made, too, a few etchings for Dickens' 'Pictures from Italy' and he contributed to three other books, but far too often his work was poorly engraved.

For almost three quarters of a century that English master of the illustrative etching, George Cruikshank, was producing superb work. The greater bulk of his work appeared in the Comic Almanac, one of the most fascinating and reliable documentaries of the early Victorian era; the best known of his etchings were made for the serialised novels of Charles Dickens. Ruskin wrote of Cruikshank's 'tragic power' and considered his lively etchings for Grimms' 'Fairy Tales' in 1824 'the finest thing next to Rembrandt done since etching was invented'.

Cruikshank always etched his own copper plates, which ensured a consistently high standard for his work. For some of his earliest designs he used aquatint, but he realised that the crisp fluid line of the etching was best suited to his humour and satire. He was an outstanding draughtsman and although he drew many hundreds of designs for wood engraving, his talent was expressed in a unique way by the etching.

In 1836 he illustrated Charles Dickens' 'Sketches by Boz', and in 1838 he made beautiful etchings for 'Oliver Twist' and 'Memoirs of Joseph Grimaldi', filled with character and humour.

The most successful illustrators have established such brilliant images that the reading public would find any variation unacceptable; such an image is Cruikshank's Fagin; every representation of him is geared to this grotesque yet pathetic demon. Charles Dickens and George Cruikshank achieved perfect harmony; both were Londoners, advocates of social reform and fascinated by distortion and the grotesque in man and nature. Other books successfully illustrated by Cruikshank's etchings were 'Peter Schlemihl' in 1824 and in 1853–4 'Cruikshank's Fairy Library'; the magic of his illustrations to 'Fairy Tales' by the Brothers Grimm was again captured in this later work.

How tame and feeble after Cruikshank's warm, lively Dickens characters do the etchings seem by 'Phiz', H. K. Browne. In 1853 he made some etchings for 'Bleak House', in 1857 for 'Little Dorrit' and in 1859 for 'A Tale of Two Cities'. All seem dispirited and lifeless and it is hardly surprising that Dickens discarded Phiz as an illustrator in 1860. Trollope, who was offered the artist's services, considered it would be impossible to find a more inferior illustrator anywhere, yet the illustrations H. K. Browne made for a number of sporting books were adequate enough, although there was little evidence of imagination or humour in any of his work.

George Cruikshank. For 'Oliver Twist'. 1838. Etching

At this time the etching was declining as a method for book illustration; the wood engraving and lithograph could be printed so much more quickly and the etching became more and more a print-making technique.

During the latter half of the nineteenth century one of the most prolific etchers was the American-born James McNeill Whistler. Trained in Paris, he came to London in 1858, where he settled, although he made frequent trips to France and Italy. His famous law suit with Ruskin resulted in the damages of one farthing being awarded to Whistler, but this seems to have given him an extraordinary amount of pleasure and certainly it ensured him public recognition. Walter Sparrow has said that Whistler won for the etching the right to sketch lightly, to leave spaces untouched. All of his work had superb atmosphere; it was delicate, often poetic, never heavy in any way.

His first twelve etchings in 1858 included 'En Plein Soleil', 'Annie Seated', 'The Kitchen', 'La Mère Gérard', 'La Vielle aux Logues'. On his arrival in London in 1858 he was greatly attracted by the Thames and the series of sixteen etchings he made in

James McNeill Whistler. View of the Thames. 1859. Etching

1871 of London's bustling shipping industry are the most exquisite of his work. Whistler's water scenes show that he was influenced by Girtin and often his shapes are not dissimilar to those of Jongkind. He made a number of very fine portraits; for some of them he used dry point; one portrait he particularly liked depicts his niece 'Annie Haden', a rather sad, elongated Victorian child. It seemed in his later work he was infected by the mood of Impressionism, but throughout his legendary career he drew spontaneously; his often exquisite designs were charming and decorative. In 1880 he published twelve etchings in his 'First Venice Set' and in 1886 'Another Venice Set'. Also in 1886 he published 'Twenty-six etchings of 1886'.

He made in all some four hundred etchings, in addition to one hundred and sixty lithographs. He selected his paper and inks meticulously and 'blanketed' his work with tedious care; this superior printing treatment contributed considerably to the exceptional quality of his etching.

In France in 1750 two outstanding artists were engraving original masterpieces, Jean-Honoré Fragonard and Gabriel de Saint Aubin. Fragonard made only four etchings, of 'Bacchanals', issued as a set, rather after the style of Tiepolo's 'Capricci', lively and charming. St. Aubin made about fifty etchings, drawn freely as were those of Fragonard, as though the plate were a sketch pad and his needle a pencil. He outlined features and highlighted faces dramatically against darkened backgrounds where shadows blurred, confused. His clusters of characters almost always communicate, his scenes have a fluidity and a rhythm, and he reflects superbly the social scene, especially the luxury-loving eighteenth-century French with time on their hands. His 'Le Salon du Louvre' of 1753 is a perfect example; crowds of bored socialites over-fill this gaunt monument, the walls are crowded in a way no gallery director would allow today, neither would dogs be permitted in so fashionable a gossip shop. 'L'Académie Particulaire' of 1760 is in his pencil-drawn style and depicts an artist drawing a somewhat resigned nude model. All of his interiors have a gaunt vastness, his lovers seem always moral and poetic and his horses are always very splendid beasts.

The landscape artist, Louis Moreau l'ainée, made a number of etchings, between 1760 and 1770, of charming countryside scenes near Paris, of cottages, bridges, trees, streams and fences; always he left large areas of the plate un-etched, providing an unusual amount of white in his prints. Moreau's etchings were published privately in two series so his work was little known in the eighteenth century, although many of his etchings were published in 1800 by Naudel at a time when landscape prints were beginning to become commercially lucrative.

In France it was an era of amateur enthusiasm for the engraved arts, made especially fashionable by the talented Madame Pompadour, mistress of Louis XV. Vivant Denon, an outstanding diplomat, made several etchings after the style of Rembrandt, as did Norblin who owned a large collection of Rembrandt prints. Boissieu, the most talented of the amateurs, made etchings influenced more by two of Rembrandt's pupils, Lievens and Van Vliet.

Line engraving was still favoured in France at the beginning of the nineteenth century; etching was little practised and etchings of quality can be picked out almost singly, as if each was the occasional experiment of an artist who favoured some other illustrative method. Ingres made a rather fine portrait of 'Gabriel Courtois de Pressigny' in 1816, a proud, dignified man of humour, very real and presumably a good likeness. The print has a silvery, luminous effect achieved only by skilful and slow biting. It is strange that Ingres did not follow this success by more portrait etching.

The only known etching of Géricault was made in 1817, 'The Dapple Grey', a more classical creature than his later lithographic horse studies.

The etchings of Eugene Delacroix were the first important contribution in nineteenth-century France. His first etchings were free copies after Rembrandt's 'Abraham and Isaac' and 'Resurrection', and among his one hundred and twenty-six etchings and lithographs were a number of aquatints which show how greatly he was influenced by Goya, especially in two prints entitled 'Interior Scene' and 'Hospital Interior'. Delacroix's aquatints are of his most exotic themes: 'Turk mounting a Horse', 'The Jewess of Algiers' dated 1833 and 'The Blacksmith' are all especially fine, full of vitality and energy. He achieved an atmosphere of menace, even in everyday scenes, at the same time they were dignified with soft effects of light and shade. He made only one etching of a nude, 'Reclining Woman seen from behind'.

Paul Huet made a large number of heavy landscape etchings reminiscent of earlier Dutch artists. His plates seem to have been bitten too deeply, his strokes were untidy and all of his scenes appear stormy, threatening in the foreground, paling to wide horizons. His 1834 'View of Avignon' might have been a lithograph, as indeed might much of his work.

Théodore Rousseau made a few landscape etchings, 'Portfolio of Six Etchings' in 1835 and 'Scree Oaks' in 1861; he achieved a mystical depth to his landscape.

Théodore Chasseriau made some very beautiful etchings. In some personal way he seems to combine the purity of Ingres and the exoticism of Delacroix with a very real sense of tragedy. In 1844 he etched fifteen plates after 'Othello', clearly bitten, dramatically posed, the characters filling a remarkable amount of the design. Perhaps they seem especially fine as almost all contemporary illustrative art seems to have been of landscape or nude studies.

Jean-Baptiste Corot was born in the eighteenth century, in 1796; he might have belonged to a later generation. Corot was one of the greatest original etchers of all time. He made fourteen etchings in addition to the sixty glass prints made by a combination of etching and daylight printing and twenty superb lithographs. His compositions are poetic masterpieces; those easy, almost careless, finely interwoven lines he used in all his work allow the imagination to define form in a personal manner, the supreme quality of Turner's organic line in reverse; both artists used their skills brilliantly to suggest definition of theme in totally different ways. Corot seems to have been influenced by the Italian landscape more in his etching than elsewhere in his work; among his etchings are 'Italian Landscape', 'Impressions of the Fortifications at Donai', 'The Duomo at Florence', 'Lake with Boatmen' and 'Wooded Landscape'. Corot achieved a serene harmony and his lines were more finely etched than those of most of his contemporaries. His earliest plate, in 1845, 'Tuscan Scene' is so beautiful, irridescent, yet it was found by Bracquemond at the bottom of a tool chest. This indifference of Corot was characteristic; he showed little interest in the printing of his work. Bound volumes of some of his etchings are magnificent collectors' pieces in the grandest manner.

Felix Bracquemond himself made a number of very beautiful etchings of birds; his seagulls in flight are superb and 'The Old Cock', not published until 1882, has the most realistic plumage. He made a number of etched portraits too.

Jean François Millet made twelve important etchings, mostly from his own paintings. His first etchings in 1855 and 1856 were of 'Sewing Woman' and 'Woman Churning'. His themes were always of gleaning, ploughing, humble domesticity. Millet, an outstanding draughtsman, greatly influenced by Rembrandt, had as delicate a touch as any artist ever had. Even when his characters are wearing the poorest clothes and the clumsiest clogs, as in that superb study 'Peasant emptying a Pail', his touch is delicate, exquisite.

One of the most prolific mid-nineteenth-century etchers was Charles Meryon. His 'Paris Scenes' of 1850 were followed by 'The Petit Pont', 'The Gallery of Notre-Dame', 'The Clock Tower', 'The Morgue'; all were drawn with vivid personality. His was a melancholy approach, and his skill may not have been exceptional, yet the etchings Meryon made between 1850 and 1854, dignified studies of sombre architecture, are of significance. 'The Morgue', one of his best known etchings, is remarkably unsinister in spite of a dead body being carried across the roof in full view of inquisitive spectators. Perhaps 'The Petit Pont' is his finest etching, a splendid unchanged façade of Paris buildings shafted in moonlight, with the towers of Notre Dame pinnacled out of perspective, the bridge and the dispirited air of a deserted waterfront. Insanity shortened the career of Meryon, yet it may also have heightened his perception and provided visionary themes such as 'Le Stryge', depicting a monster mocking the Tower of St. Jacques.

Rodolphe Bresdin, as solitary a figure as Meryon, thought the true artist should never be concerned with nature; he seems to have been incapable of drawing any aspect of realism. His imagination festered with fantasy, yet even his most mysterious themes are not macabre. He drew with precise detail, in marvellous contrasts of light. All his art was graphic and the strange scenes he envisaged are unique. 'Death's Jest Book' is one of the most strange; a man at his ending place, by the river, surrounded by evidence of death; skulls and weird bystanders watch from the clouds, trees, the bank. His etching 'The Peacocks' in 1869, a study of several peacocks perched upon branches, has a background much as Beardsley or some other *fin-de-siècle* artist might have drawn. Perhaps like Beardsley, Bresdin, too, was influenced by Japanese artists' woodcuts. Water and rocks appear in many of his studies, as in 'Nymphs Bathing'. He never varied his style for etching or lithography; he covered each plate with dots, light flared across his foregrounds in contrast to a massed, detailed background. His last etching, 'My Dream', made when he was sixty, might have been made forty years earlier; rarely does one encounter an artist with so consistent a style.

A Paris friend of Whistler and perhaps the most prolific etcher during the mid-nineteenth century was Alphonse Legros. Both Legros and Whistler were hostile to the over-etched plate although in his battle scenes, such as 'Le Triomphe de la Mort', Legros may be accused of excessive etching. However, he and Whistler settled in England, where a freer style of etching was better received. Legros made more than six hundred prints, of which more than five hundred were etchings, eight aquatints and fifty dry-points. Legros considered two-thirds of his work should have been destroyed, but he was a ruthless self-critic. Giotto influenced him, as did those master painters who had rejected themes of prettiness, such as Dürer, Holbein, Michelangelo and Mantegna. He had a close sympathy with social outcasts and a preoccupation with death; one particularly effective etching he made which combined the two he called 'La Mort du Vagabond'. His compositions were entirely without frills, his backgrounds more often than not received no treatment at all, but he could produce the most devastating effects of rain and storm. His later landscapes are gentler, almost innocuous.

With Ingres, Legros was perhaps the finest engraver of portraits. 'Auguste Rodin', 'Victor Hugo', 'Cardinal Manning' and 'Dalou' are among his finest studies; the sad, thoughtful faces receive superbly relevant strokes, the clothes are merely outlined. Legros made eight etchings as illustrations to some stories by Edgar Allen Poe; neither the stories nor the illustrations were particularly distinguished.

In 1862, Baudelaire wrote 'Etching is in fashion'. Artists he mentioned included Legros, Meryon, Manet, Ribot, Whistler and Jongkind. Not surprisingly, he stresses the function, skill and commercial enterprise of print publishers such as Cadart. Lalanne produced a textbook on etching filled with uninspired plates. But perhaps the most significant feature of the commercial revival of the etching was the founding by Cadart in 1862 of the Société des Aquafortistes. If the contributors to the Etching Club in England disappointed, the list of artists collaborating with the Société reads like some catalogue of nineteenth-century master-painters.

Perhaps the stronghold of the wood engraving and lithograph on magazine publication was too well established for the etching to remain long in fashion, although there is evidence that a great many fine artists were making etchings, either for their own pleasure or as preliminaries before or studies after their own paintings. In an effort to present a brighter image the Société changed its name in 1868 to 'L'Illumination Nouvelle' and as such it appeared until 1881. Many of the artists contributing to the Société's journal were making etchings too for 'L'Eau-forte Moderne', 'La Gazette des Beaux-Arts', 'Art' and 'Artiste'. 'L'Image', one of the liveliest periodicals, was more interested in wood engraving. In 1889 Bracquemond and Guérart made a final effort to unite those interested in the etching, to centralise the efforts of artists, collectors, critics, publishers, printers and booksellers. Their effort came too late, at a time when reproductive etching was supplanting autographic processes.

Before the original etching of the Impressionists in the last half of the nineteenth century, etchings appeared little in books other than as borders, frontispieces, vignettes. Celestin-Nanteuil used a pseudo-Gothic border and clumsy, ill-defined initial letters to a number of Victor Hugo stories, almost a decorative use. Tony Johannot used etching in some of his later work. 'Sonnets et Eaux-Fortes', published in 1869, contained the illustrations of no fewer than forty-two artists; almost as many poets contributed the poems. Doré and Manet both contributed etchings to this volume, but it is too varied in style and diverse in theme to be successful.

Édouard Manet's first work as a book illustrator was six etched plates, in addition to two vignettes for title-page and end-piece, for Charles Cros' 'Le Fleuve' in 1874, a sixteen-page poem in rhymed couplets describing the course of a river from mountain glacier through a great city, down to the sea. Only one hundred quarto copies, superbly printed, were published in addition to a few review copies. Manet's etchings are simplified almost to abstraction, in fact every aspect of the book is modern; it might easily have been published in the 1930's.

Manet made seventy-five etchings and twenty-one lithographs. His etchings were more concerned with colour and spontaneity than with the line itself. His first set of etchings in 1862 must have astonished a French print-buying public familiar with countless landscape, architectural and portrait studies.

Other artists who contributed etchings of quality from the middle of the nineteenth century include a Daubigny, who with Jongkind was a forerunner of the Impressionists; Decamps, a prolific showman, skilled but unimaginative; Eugene Lami, who contributed many vignettes, frontispieces, tail-pieces and ornamental letters, a very fine decorative artist; Ernest Meissonier, who made pleasing etchings with unusual, romantic trees; Felix Buhot, who at first drew charming harbour scenes and, after trips to England and Volognes, superb city scenes; Buhot used symbolic themes too, such as 'Genius of Dead Towns'. Theodule Ribot, influenced both by Rembrandt and the Spanish School, made dramatic use of chiaroscuro; he concentrated light on hands and faces. His themes were of interior figures and of still-life.

It was in 1855 that Edgar Degas made his first etching, a half-length, totally appealing self-portrait. Careful cross-hatching shows classical influence, yet he manages to produce a pleasing personal effect. Degas too was influenced by Rembrandt—and who was not?, even unconsciously—and he searched continually for perfection. He pulled state after state, listened and acted upon advice from friends including Manet. Degas said 'no art is less spontaneous than my own', yet his drawing seems entirely spontaneous and his poses have a marvellous rhythm. For his etching in 1870 'At the Louvre' he made twenty states; the 1865 etching of 'Marguerite de Gas' seems to have pleased him sooner. He combined dry-point with a grained etching in 1875 for 'Dancers', a theme that was to make him immortal. Degas made superb theatrical use of the spot-light and revived an interest in soft-ground etching. Anything new fascinated him; continually he experimented, re-touched, re-worked, and re-examined most of his sixty etchings, aquatints and lithographs. Most of the results are as near perfection as an artist could hope to achieve.

During the 1870's and 1880's etching was practised extensively in France. Etchings were included in periodicals, although in fewer numbers than wood engravings or lithographs; more often they were included as prints enclosed within the magazine, and, of course, prints were being sought eagerly for room decoration throughout these twenty years.

The work of Albert Besnard is familiar; he met Legros on a visit to London in 1879 and was encouraged to try etching himself. 'Portrait of Madame Besnard' in 1877, 'The

Silk Dress' in 1877, and in 1880 'The End of it All', the laying-out of a dead man, are among his sympathetic, almost paint-like studies. 'The Sick Mother', etched in 1889, is a classroom favourite; sentimental, comfortingly natural; the sick mother is bathed in light, the two children extraordinarily alive, totally unaware of probable loss. Besnard had a distinctive touch even though his style varies from strongly incised to lightly etched lines; he liked to pose his characters with their backs to the light, his organic

Edgar Degas.
Self-portrait. 1855.
Etching

lines often were stronger than those infilling; sometimes he used dry-point with etching, almost always he achieved a sheen and a paint-like quality, most especially in his portraits.

Alfred Sisley made only four etchings, entitled 'The Banks of the Loing', delicate open designs involving little drawing. Mary Cassatt made two hundred engravings and etchings, many of them influenced by the Japanese woodcutters Utamaro and Hokusai. Many of her subjects are women and children, happy, intimate scenes of little depth. James Ensor, strongly influenced by Bresdin and Redon, made one hundred and fifty engravings and etchings, filled with imaginative fantasy. Roger-Marx has said that Ensor had a profound influence upon Belgian surrealism, that he inspired a new generation of artists. His etchings include 'Skeletons warming Themselves'; 'Skeleton in the Studio'; a magnificent set from the New Testament, and best known, 'The Cathedral', a swarming multitude of crowded faces, very Flemish in feeling.

Camille Pissaro, like Degas, constantly revised his plates; sometimes the entire composition would be altered. He pulled up to sixteen states for each etching and changed both stresses and attitudes. He was strongly influenced by Corot and Millet. In 1874 he etched a portrait of Cézanne, superbly forceful. Aquatint sometimes heightened the tone of his etchings. Many of his landscapes are simple masterpieces and it is sad that to economise he etched many of his plates on zinc, which lessened the crispness of impact. In 1890 he made a coloured etching 'Church and Farm at Eragny', a stormy, sunlit scene with roofs, spire and cows, rather angular but characteristic of his work. It might quite easily be attributable to more recent artists.

Renoir made a few etchings, among them 'Two Girls Bathing' in 1895 and 'Berthe Morison'; also he etched a frontispiece for Mallarmé's 'Pages' in 1891. What beautiful book illustrations Renoir could have made—his use of colour and life made etching quite a new art.

Van Gogh seems to have made only one etching, a portrait of 'Dr. Gachet' in a strangely striking style, almost as if he had drawn it twice.

Many late-nineteenth-century artists were using dry-point for portraiture—again the genius of Rembrandt encouraged them to experiment. Whistler was commuting between France and England and his work must have been an indication of the potential of the dry-point in portraiture too. Pissaro used dry-point as early as 1881 and in 1885 Rodin used it for his striking portrait of Victor Hugo. James Ensor used dry-point frequently, as did Edouard Vuillard. It can appear rather brittle and many artists have combined its use with aquatint to soften this effect.

I have mentioned several times the influence of the Dutchman Jongkind on landscape and seascape artists throughout Europe. Jongkind made thirty etchings, drawn with a vital yet almost nervous stroke. Many of his strokes seem as improbable, as hasty and unfinished as those of Corot, but Jongkind's shapes were more specifically defined. In 1862 he issued his first portfolio of etchings, mostly landscapes of Holland and Belgium.

What a remarkable year for the etching was 1862. Artists seem to have been compelled towards it throughout Europe. Later Jongkind made a series of etchings of the Normandy coast and a third series of Paris street scenes. Often he made etched sketches preliminary to his painting, sometimes of paintings already completed. He was another master of the organic line; his roofs, sails, harbours, rivers, broads, canals, windmills, all make beautiful shapes and consciously show a debt to Rembrandt, never more so than in 'Boat at its Moorings'. Jongkind came closest to Rembrandt's subordination of any planning to the whole effect, to his intensity of vibration and movement. The Jongkind etching 'Sunset at Antwerp' in 1869 is probably his best known work; it dazzles with life; the sky, the water and boat are all as light as air. His 1863 etching 'Leaving the Port of Honfleur' was drawn more conventionally, a rather chilled, desolate waterfront, animated superbly by yachts and rowing-boat, reflective and positive. What marvellous children's book illustrations Jongkind could have made—it is easy to invent stories of animated boats merely by witnessing his warm visual characterisation.

In Germany the use of the illustrative methods and book production was developing much as it was in England and France. Artists seemed to commute as funds and inclination allowed, yet there were fewer German etchers and little use of the etching in book illustration. Many of the great German literary classics of Gessner, Schiller and Lessing were illustrated by artists throughout Europe, but the method was invariably line engraving. But many such classics had vignettes and the artist who seems to have made most of them was Chodowiecki, who made almost three thousand etchings during his lifetime. His first series before 1770 were medium sized, of conventional, rather unremarkable quality. His painting too, including a number of portraits, was also rather dull, but towards the end of the nineteenth century his etchings established him as an important illustrator of books and almanacs. Ironically, it is his earlier work that is to be found most easily; portraits of 'Frederick II on Horseback', 'Frederica Sophia', 'Wilhemina' and 'Passe-dix', depicting the Frenchman Nicolas Foinvelle, frequenter of smoking dens. In 1768 he made a large etching after his own painting of 'Calas' Last

Farewell', depicting the wrongly accused Calas leaving his fond family for prison, very much after the style of Hogarth. Voltaire campaigned public support for Calas and the Chodowiecki painting, etching and, later, a dry-point too ensured public recognition for the artist. His etching of 'Galitzine at the Battle of Choczin' in 1769 is a dramatic, striking design, filled with action and dignity, lightly etched; but it is his fond, intimate groups which are most pleasing.

Chodowiecki's style as a book illustrator was more that of a conventional vignettist. His vignettes are as elegant as those of French artists but less frivolous, and like Hogarth he liked to present a moral theme. Goethe found the good-versus-evil morality of his drawing especially commendable. His illustrations for the German classics and of those of Voltaire, Lesage, Rousseau, Beaumarchais, Cervantes, Shakespeare, Sterne and Goldsmith include some very original designs; they are often delicate, lively, always charming and sometimes very amusing. His vignettes and illustrations adorn; never do they overwhelm as they so often did in England and France at that time.

The etchings of Ambrosius Gabler deserve mention if only for their unique concept of light, shown especially well in 'Edge of the Wood'; it was as if his themes were lighted from behind.

Adolph Menzel, in addition to his brilliant wood engravings, again produced great art in his etchings for 'The Asylum' in 1844, the most emotion-charged drawings any artist has extracted from the etched plate. The faces of his disturbed inmates are difficult to forget. Menzel made several etchings up to the end of the nineteenth century. 'The

Adolph Friedrich Menzel. Studies for 'The Asylum'. 1844. Etching

Last Treasure', etched in 1895, show that even at the end of his life he could express emotion as superbly as any artist ever has.

There remain the etchings of Francisco Goya, the most significant between Rembrandt and Picasso. The Spaniard, who lived from 1746 to 1828, was impelled towards etching by loneliness; he etched to amuse himself. The caricature of Hogarth infected all Europe and the printed cartoon was enjoying a journalistic freedom paint never had; but politics and manners are so often a passing scene and it is more than probable that Goya thought little of the durability of his work. The style of his religious painting and portraiture for all its splendour was rather conventional, yet his cartoon style is often overpolished, a sophisticated presentation of raw material unhampered by ornamentation, traditions or allurement. Goya himself said that every work from his art was a synthesis; he broke from tradition, he distorted and the characters he drew were puppets, not people; they reveal, they do not feel. He was obsessed by extremes of human cruelty and suffering; every aspect of his intense passion is caricatured in his cartoons.

His first set of twenty-four etched plates, issued in 1799, 'Caprichos', followed by many more of these brilliant captions, was introduced by Goya as 'some of the many extravagances and errors that are to be found in any civilised society'. His themes were of dreams, of fantasy, violence and greed; his demon characters were used as if familiars in the world of sorcery. Sometimes he added commentary to his caption, as he did to 'Prosperous Journey'; underneath he wrote 'Where is this hellish company going, filling the air with its cries?'.

Goya had several styles of etching; he used brush, crayon and pen. Often his strokes were short and vigorous, never over-many of them; in this he was influenced by Tiepolo. Some of his etchings are soft, darkened, almost smudged; others are crisp like a pen drawing; to achieve tone and to soften the line, he often combined aquatint with the etching.

In 1810 he made a series of etchings, 'Disasters of War', but by then his work was denied publication and these prints remained censored until after his death. The movement and attack in the 'Caprichos' had given way in 'Disasters of War' to a kind of stunned immobility; his episodes of war and famine presented a defeated despair. One of the great advantages of the etching is its ability to detach the solitary figure from its environment; Goya made superb use of this quality.

'Disparates', the darkest series of all, also censored during Goya's lifetime, offer to posterity a courageous documentary of human bondage in quite remarkable contrast

Francisco de Goya. Capricho 55: 'Til Death. 1799. Etching

to his work as a painter to the Royal Court; there his portraits gave little indication that their artist might ever rebuke hierarchy.

Towards the end of his life Goya made twenty-four etchings of bull-fights filled with vivid action, but by then his fading sight was making work difficult. He found the lithograph less arduous and the finest of his bull-fighting scenes are lithographs.

For an art where the final result must be imagined rather than composed, it is surprising that the etching has several significant advantages over other illustrative methods. To portray organic line it cannot be surpassed; to illustrate the supernatural or uncanny, no other method can achieve better atmosphere, and in the hands of a great artist it can give insistent dimensional quality to a central theme, especially an isolated one, and expressive realism in portraiture.

But as an illustrative method in terms of the book, the etching was abandoned during the nineteenth century for all but limited or small editions, giving way to letterpress or lithography, both very much quicker printing methods.

5. The Engraving, 1750–1900

IT is probable that most books published during the eighteenth century were illustrated with engravings. True that it was known as the age of the vignette and that most vignettes were in fact etchings, invariably worked over by the burin afterwards, but in the more usual interpretation of illustration relating to text, the method was engraving. Any book published at that time without illustration was hardly likely to achieve financial success. Books were bought primarily for their illustrations; the typography was indifferent and indeed so it remained with little exception until this century.

Throughout the eighteenth century the engraved book illustration was often in clumsy association with the woodcut, used for ornamentation of borders and initials. By the nineteenth century Thomas Bewick had released the book from this ill-defined use of the woodcut by his inventive method of cutting the wood block; and after the delicate possibilities of the wood engraving had been discovered, the comparatively rough, un-polished quality of the woodcut, previously considered acceptable by publishers if by no one else, could be no longer tolerated.

So in terms of copper engraving, any survey of illustration must be concerned with designs of quality from a huge bulk of book and print illustration. In addition to the numbers of sets of classics and the vast volumes of engravings of details of buildings, architectural splendours and travels abroad by painter-architects, very few illustrations of original quality emerge from the flowing, flowery monotony. Far too many of the literary classics of this century and a half were illustrated deplorably, and any attempt to compare illustrations of the same book by a number of artists, reveals the casual disregard and lack of feeling many illustrators had for the text. It must be remembered, of course, that literary quality now considered 'classic' was to the artist then merely another new novel.

Nevertheless it is this excess of the sub-standard that distinguishes the illustration of exceptional quality which can compel the reader towards the text from superb visual interpretation.

The engraved illustration had a supreme significance during the eighteenth century if only because the lithograph and the wood engraving had not yet been invented. To assess national differences between England and other European countries, one might begin with William Hogarth, who contributed unique character to English art. Hogarth lived between 1697 and 1764 and he achieved greater success and fame as an engraver than as a painter. We know that he engraved coats of arms on silver plate early in his life and it is not difficult to imagine that the satirical, moral individuality of his humour tempted him to engrave designs of his own on to copper plate. Much of his best work was engraved before 1750, including 'The Rake's Progress' in 1735; 'Distressed Poet' in 1736; and 'Morning, Noon, Night and Evening' in 1741. His prints established the right for the individual to argue and to attack Establishment and rebuke injustice, and it is hardly surprising that his work was immediately popular with the print-buying public and influenced artists throughout Europe. Hogarth had a superb sense of the ridiculous and if his approach was pious and over-moral, if his prints spelled out his message rather too obviously, he made an important break-through for criticism publicly expressed. There is a monotony, a rather careless, ill-defined quality about his style, but we know that he considered the fine engraving feeble and unfeeling. His pioneer caricature, considered with the etching, gave English graphic art a characteristic which was admired and envied throughout Europe and certainly no other eighteenth-century English artist achieved such popular recognition.

Most of Hogarth's prints had neatly engraved verses printed below the design. The verse beneath the first of his engravings to be printed after 1750, 'Beer Street', published in 1751, convinces that Hogarth was one of the most conscientious of illustrators, in the strictly literal sense of the word, of all time.

It is interesting to note that piracy of his designs led Hogarth to seek an Act of Parliament in 1735 to protect the commercial potential of his prints. Each of the prints published after this date bears 'published according to Act of Parliament' engraved below the design. The characters drawn by Hogarth have slightly fatuous faces; they are frequently decaying in scenes of idleness and depravity; often they are crowded together to give emphasis to his point.

It would be difficult to imagine more unpleasant compositions than his 'Four Stages of Cruelty', which in the absence of any trade engraver's mark, seem to have been engraved by Hogarth himself. These prints are undated but they were re-issued many times and seem to have achieved popular appeal as original, if sadistic compositions.

Hogarth's prints were bound together in a number of different ways with an

William Hogarth. The Cockpit. 1759. Engraving

James Gillray. A March to the Bank. 1787. Engraving

introductory text, although the bound volumes were of little public interest to the many thousands of non-book buyers who liked his prints. Hogarth is credited also with some vignettes for editions of 'Tristram Shandy' and 'Tom Jones'.

The coarseness of Hogarth's stand against convention was in total contrast to the beautiful, elegant books published for the connoisseur in France. In England, too, the most splendid volumes were being published; many of them are very similar in appearance, folio sized, handsomely bound in leather with a good deal of gold tooling, heavy and bulky, nevertheless fascinating browsing books. Their content concerns the travels to some historically significant site and buildings, or drawings after paintings by the finest artists; this in itself entailed a considerable amount of travelling from one European country to another and must have made fascinating study before the days of the camera.

'Ruins of Palmyra', published in London in 1753, is an 'account of the voyage of two gentlemen which took them to the most remarkable places of antiquity on the coast of the Mediterranean'; the account, 'confined merely to that state of decay in which we found those ruins in the year 1751', was an 'attempt to satisfy curiosity about when and by whom built, singularity of situation, separated from the rest of mankind by an uninhabitable desert and the sources of riches necessary to support such magnificence'. This lengthy title-page indicates the purpose and scope of these remarkably lavish publications. The plates which filled the volumes were of city views, specifically designated buildings and geometrical plans all engraved with extraordinary clarity. The drawings in this particular volume were 'by Mr. Stewart and Mr. Revet, two English painters found at Rome'.

Often these splendid tomes were dedicated to the Sovereign; the 'Ruins of Spalatro' in 1764 were proudly offered to George III. Each of such volumes included a list of subscribers, the means by which they were financed.

William Chambers' 'Plans, elevations, sections and perspective views of the Gardens and Buildings at Kew in Surrey; the seat of HRH the Princess Dowager of Wales', to whom it was dedicated, was the most favoured type of luxury publication of the eighteenth century. The insular English appreciated the chance to see the splendours from other countries, but accounts of the most beautiful country houses in England they took to their hearts. Chambers was the Royal Architect and his plates depicted not only the Plans of the Palace at Kew, but all the room hangings, tapestries, portraits and outbuildings, which included aviary, menagerie and even ruins in the garden. One curious section, but by no means an uncommon inclusion in such books, details the directions to the binder.

Another royal dedication was Stuart's 'Athens' published in four volumes between 1762 and 1816, describing the antiquities of Athens and 'measured and delineated by James Stuart and Nicholas Revet', the same pair of painter-architects who collaborated to produce the drawings for 'Ruins of Palmyra'. Their names are seen so often it is hardly surprising they were designated 'found at Rome'; their services seem to have been continually in use in Greece or Italy. Usually the engravings in such volumes were prefaced by an account of the travels leading to such studies.

It would have been considered unthinkable at that time for an architect to have been less than a competent painter, but in illustrative terms these massive, workmanlike collections of drawings by architects are dull, flat and only of factual interest when compared to the visual excitement achieved by a great artist such as Piranesi. Architectural studies and views both may be, but what joy and relief one feels to discover buildings with life and light and animated use of tone.

*The Ruins of
Palmyra. Table
XVIII. 1753.
Engraving*

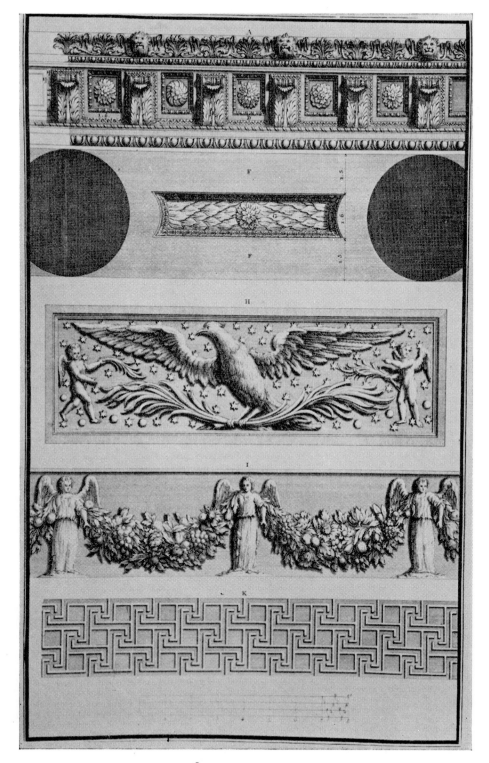

The Ruins of Balbec. Table XXIV. 1757. Engraving

84

It seems strange that the Gothic Revival should have so revolutionised architecture in the eighteenth century in England and have affected illustration so little. In France and Germany at this time there was a rather oppressive use of neo-classicism in typography as well as in illustration. Mercifully, English publishers seem to have avoided many unpleasing fashionable excesses. Even the outstanding excess of the eighteenth century, the vignette, received more sensitive handling in England than in France and Germany.

Luxury books of travel and architectural studies published at that time are to be found in large numbers. In a minority, but nevertheless in significant quantity, were equally splendid volumes filled with engravings after paintings or other *objets d'art*. One of the most magnificent books is the miscellany, 'Specimens of the Ancient Sculpture and Painting now remaining in this Kingdom from the earliest period to the reign of Henry VIII; consisting of statues, Bas Reliefs, brasses, paintings including those on glass and on walls', published in two volumes, the first in 1780 the second in 1786, by John Carter who also engraved the plates. The work was dedicated to Horace Walpole and includes some beautifully coloured engravings which in no way lessen or complicate the clarity of the drawings. The illustrations are clearly linked to the text and the historical content of such superbly varied elements from every kind of public building is as accurate today as when the plates were engraved.

Another outstanding and very much smaller set of books of the same period was the four published in two series of two volumes each in 1785 and 1788, 'Heads of Lectures on the Polite Arts' by Francis Fitzgerald, Drawing Master. The Lectures, more usually known as 'The Artists Repository', are concerned with perspective architecture, landscape, anatomy, colours and materials; they are interspersed with many engraved plates of supreme quality, almost always immediately facing the relevant text. One of the most exceptional plates is of the Pantheon at Rome, including a perspective elevation. Many of the plates are circular or oval and the engravings are in soft sepia. Volume IV has an exquisite coloured frontispiece entitled 'Rose and Jasmine': and here and there among the lectures, cherubs are used to illustrate drawing principles. All four volumes provide fascinating reading and looking. It would be impossible to find more beautifully made books than this set; even the quality of the type is superb.

Anyone who has visited an antiquarian book fair or saleroom will know that these few samples of finely illustrated books are matched by hundreds more and, in addition to those published as an edition, collectors have bound into volumes prints or even original drawings stuck in scrap-book fashion; the work of Charles Keene and David Cox is often seen in this form, especially David Cox's 'Treatise of Landscape Painting', published in 1814. Twentieth-century typography is certainly of a far higher quality, but who can imagine that many of the books published today might become fascinating collectors' pieces in a century or two; too few of them evoke the persuasion of possession.

All histories of illustration include the Baskerville edition of 'Orlando Furioso' of 1773 as a 'sample of supreme quality in English engraving', to be compared with the finest work published in France. This book is certainly fine and the illustrations are soft, flowing compositions. Another especially fine book is the Baskerville 'Select Fables of Aesop' published in 1761. Each plate has twelve minute pictures on it, miracles of expressive clarity; the typography, as might be expected from Baskerville, is much above average.

The 1786 edition of Shakespeare, organised by a man curiously always referred to as Alderman Boydell, was a mammoth nine-volumed publication, filled with engravings by most of the well-known painters of the day, including Reynolds, West, Fuseli and Romney. Their painted designs first hung as gallery exhibits before being engraved; some were mezzotinted. But the illustrations can hardly be said to be successful; the large paintings have diminished impact as engravings; too little of the engraving is sufficiently defined and the illustration is too often concerned with presenting characters in situations uninvolved with any part of the text.

It is a distressing truth that the English literary classics were better illustrated by French artists during the eighteenth and nineteenth centuries. The engravings of quality in novels now considered classic during the second half of the eighteenth century were made invariably by the artists Gravelot, Eisen, the younger Moreau or Cochin. So many novels had engravings by several artists, each with his own, often inadequate text interpretation; the paper was thin, the typography and printing indifferent and inconsistent, and by present-day standards of book production it seems remarkable that such books were so readily bought and enthusiastically read.

The caricature introduced by Hogarth was extended by Rowlandson and Gillray, considered in some detail with etching. Both made a number of engravings although the direct, crisp line of the etching was more suited to their visual humour and, if they required to soften the line, they used the burin on the plate afterwards or combined aquatint with etching.

William Blake, the only exceptional artist to produce illustrations by all known methods, made a remarkable contribution to the art by engraving the text directly on to the plate. Each line or two of the engraved text was surrounded by flowing forms, tenuously associated. Blake considered himself to be a visionary and he wrote 'a vision is not a vague vapour of non-entity; it is organised and articulated with precision, beyond all that mortal and perishable nature can produce'. His best work was undoubtedly his wood engravings and his most impressive work those relief etchings where he etched away the entire background and printed from that part of the copper plate left raised.

In 1793 Blake engraved on small metal plates a series of 'emblems' known as 'For Children; The Gates of Paradise', deceptively simple drawings entitled 'Fire', 'Air', 'Help', 'Earth' and 'Aged Ignorance' and many other such fancies. 'I want, I want', depicting a ladder to the moon, is an especially delightful composition.

In 1797 he made a large number of water-colour illustrations for Young's 'Night Thoughts', some of which were engraved and published. In 1802 Blake made some engravings for a book of ballads; the designs are pleasant enough but it is difficult to find their relevance to the poems. The engraved plate he made for Chaucer's 'Canterbury Tales' in 1809 was a total failure; Blake seems to have been incapable of subordinating his own fertile imagination to an existing text.

The middle years of Blake's career were spent relief-etching and wood engraving, although he returned to line engraving towards the end of his life. His twenty-two engraved plates for 'The Illustrations of the Book of Job' are considered by many to be the highlight of his career; for these he used wide, regular borders. Sometimes he engraved lines of text in these borders, but the book was never published although some years later a limited edition of his bound engravings was published. Blake completed only seven of the plates for Dante's 'Inferno' before he died; again the illustrations seem more concerned with his own interpretation than with Dante's story.

By the beginning of the nineteenth century many books were published with mezzotint illustrations. Certainly the best known book to include mezzotints was the Boydell Shakespeare. Mezzotint was more popular in England than elsewhere in Europe, where it was called 'manière Anglaise'. Those famous Reynolds mezzotint prints after his own paintings and portraits established a successful example for the engraver to follow; some of the Reynolds paintings were mezzotinted in monochrome with success. Without question, mezzotint reproduces oil paintings superbly, better than any other illustrative method.

During the 1820's and 1830's one of the finest English landscape painters, Constable, had many of his landscape sketches mezzotinted. John Martin used mezzotint too for Milton's 'Paradise Lost' in 1824 and for an edition of the Bible between 1831 and 1835. After the peaceful brilliance of Turner and Constable, the Martin designs seem rather alarming; melodramatic, grotesque, often over-exposed, almost lurid in character. It is little wonder that John Martin is often considered a pre-runner of surrealism.

Turner, another of the great English landscape painters, used mezzotint for book illustrations, although normally he prefered them to be printed from a steel rather than a copper plate. His seventy-one etched plates for 'Liber Studiorum' included many designs subsequently mezzotinted by trade engravers. Between 1824 and 1830 he made some drawings for steel-engraved mezzotints for 'Rivers of England', a beautiful volume, as was 'Rivers of France' published between 1833 and 1835, which included line engravings by Turner. He drew the most exquisite, detailed vignettes, which were also printed from steel, to illustrate many books of poems, including those by Byron, Scott and Milton.

The Turner vignettes and small engravings for Roger's 'Italy' are perhaps the best of his illustrative work; they are so perfectly assimilated with the text and the degree of detail, in so small a space, is very skilful. It is difficult to remember that steel engraving is essentially a line process when one sees the soft, delicate compositions Turner achieved. Sometimes colour was added after his engravings were printed; gently washed tone, always under-played and completely natural.

Steel engraving is said to have been innovated in or around 1823. The steel-engraved print is crisp with a hard brilliance, a luminosity; the most exquisite designs can be printed with such delicacy and any foliage or natural feature seems to have been touched by frost.

One of the finest books ever to include steel engravings was 'Coast Scenery' by Clarkson Stanfield, published in 1836. Tremendous seas and stormy, threatening skies are beautifully moving. Yet it remains essentially a superb but chilling book, as if one has entered a vast unheated building just before opening it.

The 'Drawing Room Scrap Book Series', published between 1830 and 1850, was illustrated mainly by steel engravings, but the designs are so minute that the text dominates and any impact is diminished.

One of the books of this period which was bound in velvet although most of the edition was leather-bound, 'Picturesque Annual', included twenty-two steel engravings among a text that provides fascinating insight into what early educated Victorians considered worthwhile Sunday reading and looking.

John Ruskin. Foreground leafage from 'Modern Painters', Vol 3. 1856. Steel engraving

Often quoted in histories of book illustration as an important book of its time, 'The Authors of England', published in 1838, included fourteen steel-engraved plates, all of them portraits.

Another annual with steel-engraved plates, 'Peter Parley's Annual', achieved only two issues in 1846 and 1847. And John Ruskin drew some exquisite compositions which were engraved on steel and included in his 'Modern Painters'.

The nature of the steel engraving demanded a far greater discipline by the artist than the line engraving, copper being so much softer a metal than steel. An artist unsure of his ability to engrave a competent organic line would certainly not have chosen the steel plate to engrave.

Any study of nineteenth-century illustration in England reveals a dominating personality in Henry Shaw, who was born in 1800 and lived for seventy-three years. He was a draughtsman of exceptional skill, not a great original artist by any standards, but his range of publications reflected an instinctive awareness of the taste and interests of Victorian readers. Most of his work was issued in parts and later bound into volumes; almost all of it was published by Pickering at the Chiswick Press. Between artist, printer and publisher, the best of Victorian illustration and book design was achieved. Many of Shaw's designs were lithographed; often he combined several methods of illustration, varying the process always for effect rather than for economy. If one of his illustrations is a lithograph or an engraving, it is so because Shaw considered the medium best for that particular design.

His earliest work seems to have been 'The History and Antiquities of the Chapel at Luton Park', a folio of twenty engravings published by James Carpenter of Old Bond Street between 1827 and 1830. His first Pickering publication, issued in parts between 1830 and 1833, 'Illuminated Ornaments selected from Manuscripts of the Middle Ages', is illustrated with etchings and lithographs, hand-coloured in addition to gold leaf.

'Specimens of Ancient Furniture' was published in parts in 1832 and in book form in 1836, and 'Specimens of the details of Elizabethan Architecture' was issued in parts during 1834 and published complete in 1839. Both included illustrations produced by a variety of engraved techniques together with some lithographs.

Also in 1836 Shaw produced 'The Encyclopedia of Ornaments', a modest forerunner of Owen Jones' magnificent 'Grammar of Ornament' illustrated by lithographs in 1856; perhaps Jones liked this book and considered it a theme deserving enlargement.

The most ambitious part-issue Shaw attempted was in 1840, 'Dresses and Decorations of the Middle Ages'; each part contained four engraved plates and some woodcuts printed in up to four colours. Published in book form in two volumes in 1843, it was a splendid production with ninety-four plates of miniatures, paintings, furnishings, stained glass and jewellery. One might justifiably claim it to be the finest English illustrated book of the nineteenth century. The Ackermann Aquatint Series and Daniell's 'Voyage around Great Britain' have illustrations of equally supreme quality, but the typography and design throughout are far superior in the Shaw book.

Other books including engravings by Shaw were 'Examples of Ornamental Metal-work' in 1839; 'Alphabets, Numerals and Devices of the Middle Ages' in 1845; and 'The Arms of the Colleges of Oxford' published in 1855. In addition he produced designs for many other books of equal merit, which were printed as etchings, wood engravings and lithographs.

Ruari McLean has said that Shaw's hand-coloured books were among the last magnificent ones produced and mark the end of a great era of 'wasteful, expensive, typical examples of the English period of genius'. Other books with engraved illustrations which McLean liked of the mid-nineteenth century were the 1859 edition of 'Poems' by Oliver Goldsmith, for which Humphreys, better known for his lithographs, produced two colour engravings; and 'The English Lakes' by Harriet Martineau, which included six steel engravings among the many wood engravings.

Copper and steel engravings continued to be made in limited numbers throughout the nineteenth century, but for book illustrations engravings were made for re-issues only where the plate was already held at the printers. It is, in fact, exceedingly difficult to find nineteenth-century books of octavo or normal reading size, with engravings; almost always the illustrations are lithographs or wood engravings.

Few English artists achieved anything like the quality of the engraved prints produced in vast quantities in France. Two exceptions who did achieve European status, Seymour Haden and James Whistler, originally an American, made many hundreds of superb etchings and some engravings. Whistler, like many other artists who drew freely with an original style, was condemned by critics, especially in Paris, where his work was rejected by the Salon. Such official disapproval in mid-nineteenth-century Paris we now consider synonymous with the fine artist; the establishment directorate of a century ago might be surprised to discover how universally despised their taste and opinions have become.

The eighteenth century in France was perhaps the most outstanding period in the history of book illustration. Not only were there great numbers of the most luxurious volumes published but literary texts from all European countries were being illustrated with sensitivity and taste by French artists. Pocket-sized volumes were being published for the first time, for light-reading; many salon tables were strewn with beautifully bound books of stories illustrated with engravings, and young ladies liked to be seen in parks and carriages carrying such pleasant divertisement.

Of course the engravings were not yet printed on the same page as the text; they were inserted here and there; even so they were often closer to the relevant text than many publishers achieve today.

In the earlier part of the eighteenth century religious and political studies had been popular forerunners of the spate of 'philosophes', so characteristic of the developing freedom of thought in pre-Revolutionary France; a great many illustrations of superfine quality had been published during the twenty years before 1750.

The first significant French artists who were drawing for reproduction in the mid-eighteenth century are Gravelot and the younger Cochin. Cochin, who came from a family of talented engravers, was probably the most prolific vignettist of the eighteenth century; his work was of fine quality, but although he lived until 1790 he produced little of note after 1750. In 1741 he began to produce frontispieces for book illustration; he preferred always to work in small, intricate scale. Diderot called Cochin 'the leading French draughtsman' and considered his work too allegoric. Yet his touch was light, delicate, almost always very pretty, even in those themes where he seemed to be obsessed with time, death, religion. The happiest of his work is to be seen in the charming compositions he made of festivals and wedding ceremonies; certainly no artist has captured gaiety more skilfully.

Hubert Gravelot, not so intensely productive an artist as Cochin, was in London for a number of years before 1745, when he returned to Paris. His engravings for several English classics are printed still today, including those he did for Gay's 'Fables' in 1738 and Richardson's 'Pamela' in 1742. Gravelot trained craftsmen to engrave his work; one of the best of these was Charles Grignion, who engraved the Bentley designs for the edition of Gray's 'Poems' in 1753. Bouchot said that the illustrations Gravelot made in England were thoroughly French, yet when he returned to France his designs were influenced by the style of Hogarth. Such contrary individualism is not difficult to understand from such a lover of life and pleasure. Gravelot's greatest success came after his return to Paris, when he made vignettes and engravings for several important books, including 'Decameron and Boccaccio' published in London in 1756; Marmontel's 'Contes' published in Paris in 1765 and 'La Nouvelle Heloise' in 1761 in Amsterdam. Many books of mid-eighteenth century bear a Dutch imprint; social and political comment was uncensored at that time in Holland, whereas in France restrictions were excessive and inhibiting. Several editions of the works of Corneille are illustrated by Gravelot engravings too at that time.

The 'Contes Moraux' of Marmontel provides the most successful example of Gravelot's book illustrations. His domestic scenes and especially those of interiors are superb, as are his stable scenes; even when his engraving shows careful cross hatching, his poses are full of rhythm and warmth. Boucher, Cochin and Eisen were also contributors to the Decameron engravings; octavo in size, this book is rather splendid and would have been more beautiful if one artist only had provided illustration designs.

Charles-Dominique Eisen.
For 'Contes de la Fontaine'.
1762.
Engraving

Charles-Dominique Eisen, the Flemish artist, produced engravings more vigorous in style than his more elegant contemporaries Cochin and Gravelot. If Gravelot was considered to be pleasure-seeking, Eisen might be said to debauch, but his quality as an artist was superb, his style sophisticated and exquisite. In 1753 he engraved a collection of decorative motives entitled 'Premier livre d'une œuvre suivi'; vignette sized, these designs have provided inspirational source for generations of decorative artists and designers.

In 1762 Eisen engraved illustrations for perhaps the most famous of all eighteenth-century books, the 'Contes' of La Fontaine. The book was sponsored by the 'fermiers generaux' or tax collectors; almost *nouveaux riches* in taste, they associated to form one of the first societies of bibliophiles; Eisen was approached to design the plates and several exquisite vignettes were contributed by Choffard. Eisen was influenced by several Flemish and Dutch artists, particularly Rubens. Several variant editions were published of this fine book: one edition included extra plates drawn by Eisen with less regard for conventional morality; another omitted the tail-pieces. As with so many books of that time, the paper is rather too thin and the typography disappointing, but nevertheless it is a beautifully illustrated book.

In 1770 Eisen provided illustrations for Dorat's 'Les Baisers'; the poetry is not worth reading, but the vignettes and fleurons are delightful if sometimes immoral. The illustrations dominate in the manner of eighteenth-century books, text being merely the pretext for illustration.

The 1767 edition of Ovid's 'Metamorphoses' included some engravings by Eisen and others by Gravelot, Moreau and Choffard, and also woodcut fleurons which provide a representative example of the clumsy association of the ornamental woodcut with engravings, especially apparent when those engravings are the delicate tail-pieces of Choffard.

The last book Eisen illustrated seems to have been Montesquieu's 'Le Temple de Guide' in 1772; the text is engraved too and the book is wholly fascinating visually. It is remarkable and significant that the author's name does not appear on the title-page!

For much of the nineteenth century, publishers dispensed altogether with the pretext of a text: they bound engravings with a title-page, an index and an occasional biographical note on the artist. Books with any significant text were soon to be bound with wood-engraved illustrations or lithographs when the engraving had become an uncommercial extravagance.

The fifty-three tail-pieces which Choffard produced for the Eisen-illustrated edition of 'Contes' of La Fontaine were the climax of a career which lasted forty years. Choffard was considered essentially an ornamenter, a designer of tail-pieces, borders and dedications. His designs were always finely drawn, of a consistently high quality if rather similar.

Marillier, who had collaborated with Eisen to produce designs for 'Les Baisers', made engravings in 1773 for another of Dorat's works, 'Fables Nouvelles'. The head and tail-pieces for this book are very pleasing, strongly decorative in style. Marillier attempted some engraved illustrations for the Bible, but his approach was insincere, almost flippant, and the results are neither convincing or successful.

Colin à mon cœur n'offre qu'une fleur,
Mais de sa constance
J'attens tout mon bonheur.

Jean-Michel Moreau le jeune. L'Aimant Timide from 'Choix de Chansons' by M. de la Borde.
1773. Engraving

Perhaps the most representative figure of the latter half of the eighteenth century in France was Jean-Michel Moreau le jeune, who continued to engrave well into the nineteenth century. His later work, neo-classical in style, is markedly inferior to his earlier work, which is graceful, filled with light and life and provides social commentary on contemporary France. One of the most beautiful books of all time, 'Choix de Chansons' by M. de la Borde, published in 1773 in four volumes, included many Moreau engravings. The engravings in the first volume are all by Moreau. The title-pages are exquisite engraved masterpieces; the human groups drawn by Moreau are marvellously alive, his elegantly gowned ladies have magnetic presence, and the plates are never overworked. Moreau achieved superb balance between ornament and design; many fine artists fail in this distinction. Moreau illustrated several of the works of Rousseau between 1774 and 1783 and his engraving of 'The Last Words of Jean-Jacques Rousseau' was a best-selling print. Another of his prints which sold in enormous numbers was 'Illuminations for the Marriage of Louis XVI', surely one of the most remarkably skilful interpretations of artificial light ever drawn.

Moreau made twenty-four engravings for another very splendid book in 1776, 'Monument du Costume', a magnificent courtly commentary on the reign of Louis XVI. In any medium there has been no greater expression of French manners than that provided by Moreau.

Jean Honoré Fragonard was primarily a painter, yet his engravings are to be found in some of the most sumptuous books ever published. His illustrations have a freshness and often an appealing frivolity. Some sixty engravings were issued as prints after his paintings, among them 'Le Chiffre d'Amour', 'La Bonne Mère' and 'The Happy Accidents of the Swing', but these are intensely worked, as though it were a sin to leave any part of the plate unengraved; other prints issued were feeble versions of his pleasing ink-and-wash drawings now in the Louvre.

Fragonard collaborated with his friend L'Abbé Saint-Nome, who sponsored the five enormous volumes of 'Le Voyage Pittoresques de Naples et de Sicile' published between 1781 and 1786, and a smaller edition of the same work entitled 'Fragments Choisis'. Almost all important private libraries seem to have this magnificent set of volumes; it is a supreme example of luxury book-making.

Fragonard produced one hundred and fifty crayon-and-wash drawings for Ariosto's 'Orlando Furioso', beautiful, soft, indeterminate designs; but they presented the engraver with an insurmountable problem and were never published.

Sicily seems to have been one of the places most frequented by artists and travellers at this time. Jean Honel, painter to the king, produced hundreds of soft, sepia engravings accompanied by fascinating diary commentary for the four-volumed 'Voyages des Isles de Sicile', published in 1782.

François Boucher, already mentioned as a contributor to the Ovid's 'Metamorphoses' of 1867–71, was best known for his engravings for the plays of Molière; but his designs were rather idyllic and posed, adequate but without originality.

Another painter-engraver, Gabriel de Saint-Aubin, a member of a remarkably talented family, was a pupil of Boucher. He made fifty plates, most of which he etched first and subsequently engraved. Saint-Aubin is considered in some detail with the etching as is Louis Moreau, the landscape artist, and the many talented amateur engravers.

Jean Baptist Simeon Chardin made some fifty engravings too, after his paintings—sentimental scenes of the middle and professional classes.

There were so many painters of talent in France at this time, and most of them made engravings for prints; none was so successful as Eisen, Cochin or Gravelot, who were not painters. Most of the engravings were of niceties, polite scenes of etiquette, such as those depicting the 'salon set' by Debucourt. The Swiss philosopher Lavater, contemporary of Debucourt, whose book 'Physiognomy' was published in German, French and English editions from 1775, used the German artist Chodowiecki to provide engraved illustrations. These heavy volumes were studies of man's moral nature as revealed in his face and countenance, and influenced many artists including Debucourt and the Swiss Jean Huber to feel that facial expression should have greater significance.

At this time, too, there were many landscape engravers who studied with Le Bas, who was responsible for a great many book illustrations, including those for Vernet's 'Ports de France'. Throughout Europe there was an almost unbelievable number of trade engravers who normally took over the artist's work after he had etched the plate. Née and Masquelier were trade engravers who specialised in landscape engraving; they were responsible for the two hundred and eighty-four engraved illustrations to Saint Nome's 'Voyage pittoresques . . .', already mentioned as including designs by Fragonard; La Borde's 'Description de la France'; Choiseul-Gouffier's 'Voyage de la Grèce' and Cassas' 'Voyage d'Istree et de Dalmatic'. Masquelier seems to have etched the designs and Née, a prolific vignettist, seems to have engraved the plates afterwards.

Engravings printed during the French Revolution inevitably attacked Establishment, and themes of elegant idleness gave way to strife and injustice. Many engravings at this time, in fact almost all of those bound into the fifty massive volumes in the Cabinet des Estampes, were printed without the names of the artists. Artists whose style was familiar produced no engravings which might be recognised; certainly it was not so lucrative an employment as it had been. In 1793 it became law to deposit each print with the Bibliothèque Nationale, and this, too, encouraged anonymity during this uneasy time of visual attack. The caricature initiated in England and extended by Rowlandson and Gillray infected European artists. Anti-clerical caricature was encouraged in France, where it was a powerful agitator, but the English cartoonists were never surpassed or even equalled in France; in fact many French artists, including Debucourt, achieved success only by imitating the style of published English cartoons.

Immediately post-Revolution in France, that great printer Pièrre Didot succeeded his father as printer of literary classics. For his quarto volumes of the works of Molière, published between 1792 and 1800, he commissioned painters rather than vignettists for the illustrations. In 1794 Didot commissioned Regnault to prepare engravings for La Fontaine's 'Adonis' and also for the famous 1796 edition of Montesquieu's 'Le Temple de Guide'. Gérard was approached to illustrate La Fontaine's 'Psyche' in 1797; Prud'hon for Gentil Bernard's 'Art d'aimer' in 1796; Gérard and Girodet for the 1799 edition of 'Virgil'.

The Didot edition of Racine included the work of eight painters and fifteen engravers. Prud'hon made only one frontispiece before irrevocable disagreement with Racine, and after this, David and some of his pupils took over the direction of the illustrative content, using a number of artists including Gérard, Girodet and Moitte.

Claude Roger-Marx has said that engraving has owed its salvation always to a combination of writers and painters. So near to extinction on many occasions during the nineteenth century, Gauthier, Baudelaire, Burty, the Brothers Goncourt, Buhot, Gérard, Roger-Marx, Lepère and finally Ambroise Vollard, in their numerous different ways, revived and re-created interest in the original engraving.

It is certainly true that the medium chosen by illustrative artists disciplined their talents, and in terms of the engraving, the lavish but somewhat monotonous use of it during the eighteenth century made it poor competition to the lithograph and the wood engraving early in the nineteenth century. Also the trade engravers were too often guilty of careless interpretation and artists too little concerned with reproduction into print.

Inevitably engraving became associated with the innocuous, such as those three volumes of Redouté, 'Les Roses', printed between 1817 and 1824; some of these were in fact stipple engravings. Later the Redouté 'Roses' were produced lithographically, but the engravings are far superior. Nevertheless the illustrations are perhaps too familiar, too associated with inferior application to ill-designed twentieth-century household trappings, and even those earlier designs seem flat and stilted.

Steel engraving, popular in England, where it was used by the finest landscape painters, was used less in France although several beautiful books with steel-engraved illustrations were published there. Tony Johannot provided some very fine steel engravings for Victor Hugo's 'Notre Dame de Paris'. Balzac's 'Peau de Chagrin' in 1838 has steel-engraved plates, or rather vignettes, within the text; Pérrault's 'Les Contes' shows superb use of the steel engraving, both for illustrations and for some of the text. So brilliant and crisp, the steel engraving had a restraining effect over Romantic exuberance too often seen at this time. The La Fontaine's 'Fables', published in 1833 with engravings by Goujet, is an example of Romanticism at its worst; to compare with the Eisen edition is to experience the best and worst that illustration can offer.

A typical nineteenth-century product was the song book, more in evidence in England, where music was a favourite Victorian family activity; but throughout Europe very beautiful designs were printed, some of them simply and elegantly. One of the most beautiful of all nineteenth-century books was 'Chants et Chansons Populaire de la France', published in 1842 with engravings by Daubigny and Meissonier. It is unbelievably exquisite with superb balance between text and illustration.

During the mid-nineteenth century, as elsewhere, the engraved book was published in limited numbers and small editions. The founding of the Société des Aquafortistes in 1863 infused life to original engraving, once more close to extinction as an original art form. It had been used exclusively by print publishers to copy painting masterpieces and far too many of these prints were engraved deplorably. Cadart, the outstanding print publisher of the mid-nineteenth century, was one of the instigators of the new society and Legros and Baudelaire were also founder members. Not surprisingly, the best of the work contributed was etching—artists had seen too much of their art spoiled by insensitive engraving—and there is no doubt that, in the hands of the great artist, the line of the etching can be magnetic.

In 1868 the Société des Aquafortistes became 'L'Illustration Nouvelle' and for another thirteen years Cadart printed engravings from a superior range of artists. Yet it was a time of tenuous fortune for the engraving still, and in 1880, Degas, Pissaro,

Cassatt and Rafaelli launched a new journal 'Du Jour et de la Nuit' in an attempt to re-establish enthusiasm. Even though it included Degas' 'At the Louvre', the new journal achieved a single issue only.

At this time the most successful original engraving was dry-point, although it was some years before it became recognised as such, and even those fine dry-point portraits of Rodin seem to have been received with little enthusiasm.

The work of the major artists of this post mid-nineteenth century in France, including that of Meryon, Millet, Corot, Whistler, Jongkind, Manet, Degas and Bresdin, has been included at some length with the etching. Most of their work was published as prints and is very familiar. We may assume that many of these artists made engravings too or designed for engravings; Degas certainly did—he tried all illustrative methods; but his most outstanding work was in etching or lithograph. It was inevitable that public indifference to engraving and the commercial success of the wood-engraved or lithographed book illustration should have emphasised to these fine painters that any graphic interpretation of their art must be of minor importance. Any one from this remarkable list would have been exceptional isolated in a less fertile period; as it is, they form an era quite unique in the history of graphic art.

Reproductive engraving was protected by another society, 'Société des Graveurs au Burin', founded in 1868 by Henriquel-Dupont, who lectured at the École des Beaux-Arts. Less ambitious and more scholarly in approach, it survived until the engraving was reproduced photographically.

The overall impression of engraving during the last part of the nineteenth century is of a number of monotonous, lifeless compositions with a dull excess of regular cross-hatching. Bracquemond singled out only one engraver from this period, Ferdinand Gaillard, who made several compelling portrait engravings. A Franciscan, his portrait of 'Dom Prosper Gueranger' is a beautiful study of a very real man, with sympathetic yet magnetic eyes. We know that Gaillard used every possible variation in technique and that he made as many as thirty states for his plates; in a sense, he built up an expression, yet when he had achieved it, the face had more emotion and feeling than most artists ever achieve. Roger-Marx described him as 'a fitting swan-song to the line engraving'.

Engraving in Germany seems to have been rather disappointing and had few participants. Adolph von Menzel is included with the etching, Chodowiecki too. Wilhelm Liebl engraved and etched some rather fine portraits, menacing and heavy but certainly alive. Probably as many impressive volumes of architectural splendours were published in Germany as in France, but no German artist emerged from the dominating skills of architect and engraver.

It is difficult to select from the vast numbers of luxury volumes published in Italy during the eighteenth century. Most of them made no attempt at even the pretext of a text and there is an impressive but overwhelming similarity among them. Perhaps the supremity of Piranesi, Canaletto and Tiepolo, with their magnificent combination of reality and imagination, further deadens the accurate skill of the architect-painters. Also the bindings of Italian books were normally less opulent than those in France and, when searching at length from one magnificent book to another, only the exceptional in every sense of book-making emerges.

'La Pitture Antiche D'Ercolano e Contro', in nine volumes, published from 1757, has the most perfect frontispiece and volume one includes the most superb map of the Bay of Naples.

'La Capella Manetti dipinta a Fresco da Giotta' is hand-painted on the title-page of this book, edited and dedicated by Thomas Patch to Bernard Manetti, a Florentine nobleman. The engravings are from the original pictures by Giotto in the Church of the Carmelites, destroyed by fire in 1771. Part two is dedicated to Sir Horace Mann, H.M. Envoy at the Court of Tuscany, and is of the life of Massacio. A portrait of Massacio is followed by twenty-five male portraits, mostly profiles. Both volumes have the text in Italian and English. Part three, dedicated to Horace Walpole, is on the Tuscan artist Bartolommeo. Part four, entitled 'Caricature', has no text at all and includes soft sepia engravings of crayon drawings of subjects as varied as costume and sculpture.

An exceptionally fine architectural sample from Italy was 'Gili ordini di Architectura del Barozzi da vignola', published by Carlo Amati in 1805. Amati was a Milanese architect and his scale drawings of pillars, plinths, arches, friezes, masonry details, ornaments and doorways are superbly drawn. The text is scholarly and painstaking and certainly the illustrations are sumptuous and exceptional.

So in Italy, as elsewhere in Europe, the purpose of eighteenth-century books was topographical, architectural, historical and to catalogue the finest works of art.

David Bland has said that American illustration derived wholly from Europe in the nineteenth century, that there was little illustration of merit in America before that time and that only in this century has it struck out in its own direction. Even so, large numbers of illustrations were printed in America and these provided vital visual communication then and social history now, not only across America but also in

Europe. Prints were brought to London during the mid-nineteenth century to be sold and they were much sought after. Most of the prints to cross the Atlantic seem to have been printed by Carington Bowles; several of them are now in the British Museum.

Many of the early illustrations in America were of engraved maps and charts, lightly colour-washed and often with some local civic building engraved neatly outside or below the map border. One of the earliest cities to be recorded in this way was Philadelphia. William Faden engraved a 'Plan of the City and Environs of Philadelphia' in 1777, with the City Statehouse drawn below a precise, almost empty map.

Paul Revere did a number of engravings of Boston and the Boston Massacre, many of them beautifully coloured. Most coloured illustrations during the eighteenth and nineteenth centuries in America appear now to be of a rich orange brown, due in part to the blues and greens fading, but more to the rich colouring of local building materials.

There is evidence everywhere that the cartoon from Europe had reached America by the mid-eighteenth century, and as early as 1754 Benjamin Franklin engraved a now famous poster of a disjointed snake with the words 'Join or Die'. 'The Bunker Hill Hair Style', engraved in 1775, was another popular illustration. The English suffered severe casualties at the Battle of Bunker Hill and this, and the Tea troubles at Boston, brought about a large number of 'boycott British' illustrations in books, periodicals, broadsheets and posters. 'England threatened by Competition' was another common theme, the engraving showing clearly the influence of Hogarth, with the drawing carefully cross-hatched and the pictures filled with diverse activity.

American illustrations of the eighteenth century were moral and patriotic, many of the engravings being ornamented with crude woodcuts; there was little of originality or any remarkable talent.

One of the earliest books with illustrations of note was Philip Astley's 'Modern Riding Master' printed in 1776, but the engravings were made from drawings; there was little original graphic art except for magazines and posters, where the illustration was largely in the form of ornament. Early American magazines were patriotic and colonial. Paul Revere was associated with the 'Royal Magazine or Universal Repository of Instruction and Amusement', which contained political material and engravings of song music, poetry; Revere made most of the twenty-two engravings in the fifteen issues published between 1774 and 1775. Almost all of the magazines had subtitles, including 'Freeholders Magazine or, Monthly Chronicle of Liberty'; 'The Pennsylvania Magazine or, American Monthly Magazine'; and 'The Massachusetts

Magazine or, Monthly Museum of Knowledge and Rational Entertainment'. Some periodicals were printed in both English and American editions to promote political opinion. Prints were advertised in newspapers and magazines, and there was much correspondence over plagiarism of themes. It was a time of enthusiasms and technical innovation, and often magazines failed after a single issue.

Artists in the eighteenth century saw America as an experimental area, and gradually, as their links with Europe became firm, so did their belief in their own permanence and the often crudely illustrated ephemera gave way to more lasting standards of illustration. Even so, little compared in quality to anything in Europe, and that which did was imitative. The cartoon flourished in America and illustrations in magazines and books were of political themes and aggression until many years after the Revolution.

Two Bibles were published in the 1790's with engravings by Amos Doolittle, but the illustrations were undistinguished and again imitative of Hogarth.

Often collections of engraved maps and views were hand coloured and bound. In 1800 William Birch published the first edition of views of Philadelphia, with twenty-nine coloured plates of civic buildings. Hundreds of interior views of cities and buildings were printed and one of their most prolific engravers was Abel Bowen. One of the most charming books published in America at the beginning of the nineteenth century was Robert Sutcliff's 'Travels in Some Parts of North America in the Years 1804–1811'. The engravings in it are like pieces of embroidery, with activity allocated evenly and unrelated.

There is a feeling of spaciousness and naïveté about American illustration especially when compared to the overfilled activity taking place in the illustrations of European artists. Some of the printed material was issued in the form of manuals such as 'Atlantic Neptune', published for the British Admiralty between 1763–1784 as a navigational guide to American waters.

Thousands of engravings of battle scenes were made and many of the best were engraved by John Norman and bound into a three-volumed set, 'An Impartial History of the War in America', published in Boston 1781–1784. An English version had been published in 1780 which makes doubtful the claim of the title of the book.

Steel replaced copper for engraving at the beginning of the nineteenth century and in 1810 Jacob Perkins produced bank-notes by steel engraving. A. B. Durand made steel engravings in 1830 for Bryant's 'The American Landscape' and also for 'Picturesque America' in 1872–4, which includes both steel and wood engravings. It is difficult to find early American illustrations of superiority, but all provide superb visual history. All kinds of documents were engraved and printed, many of them exuding emotional patriotism. Large numbers of them can be seen in the New York Public Library and in State Archive Depositories.

In America, as in Europe, more lavish social documentation has never been provided, but little of such documentation was in any way expressive of the living, the freely expressed, the original or imaginative. Accurate imitative illustration inevitably must expire. We can be thankful that, by the latter part of the nineteenth century, artists associated themselves with Naturalism, Symbolism, Impressionism and Expressionism, movements suggesting life and optimism; and, above all, that they illustrated not only what they saw with their eyes but what they felt from within themselves.

6. The Lithograph, 1800–1900

ALOIS SENEFELDER patented his discovery of five years earlier, in London in 1801, and from that time 'Polyautography', as his process was known, until it was renamed Lithography in France in 1803, was printed from a press in London. Senefelder himself offered instruction on the technique and use of materials during that first year, ensuring an opportunity and quality which surpassed that anywhere in Europe. During the first twenty years of lithography Senefelder made many improvements to his process, which he described in an authoritative book published in 1818. The accuracy of his assessment of the limitations and future possibilities of the lithograph make it a remarkable work. Senefelder saw lithography as only one form of chemical printing and he did not minimise the advantages of using a flat surface to produce an effect inimitable by any other process. The 'crayon manner' enabled an artist to multiply his original drawings; the 'transfer manner' enabled him to transfer drawings on paper to stone. Both methods, using a greasy ink, gave to the artist a new independence, where his art was no longer allied to the efficiency and sensitivity of the engraver.

Alois Senefelder. Landscape with Gate and Round Tower. 1799. Lithograph

Senefelder remained in London for only seven months, selling his patent for three thousand pounds to Philipp André, who took over the London press. André directed his efforts to promoting lithography as a graphic art; he approached the best artists of the day to encourage them to try the new medium. The public at that time favoured water-colour paintings and the indifference to this exciting new process led André to publicise it with clear, neat images; cross hatching, crisp pen strokes and a well-defined use of black and white imitated the effects of the engraving and the etching. Blake, the one English artist who might have used lithography extensively with beauty and originality, was out of London during André's activity; in any case he was committed to the style of his Prophetic books at that time. The few lithographs Blake did make, especially one he called 'The River of Life', gives an indication of how successfully he might have developed the freedom of the process to his flowing style. Addison, writing in the 'Spectator' (No. 166), stated, 'all other graphic mediums require special training and discipline and do not allow the freedom and spontaneity of drawing with pen or crayon'. Perhaps it was this very freedom which discouraged English artists from experimentation, as if the ease of reproducing their drawing into print might prostitute their art. Certainly disrespect for the lithograph remained throughout the century. In 1857 John Ruskin wrote 'let no lithographic work come into this house', yet a few years earlier some of his own designs for 'The Stones of Venice' had been lithographed by Boys.

During the first years of lithography several pleasing drawings, in both pen and crayon, were made and the publication of each contributed to the progress and development of the process. While in London in 1801, Senefelder supervised the printing of some crayon drawings by Conrad Gessner, son of the poet; when he returned to Germany, Senefelder took these with him as samples. Also in 1801, Benjamin West, the American-born President of the Royal Academy, made the first important lithographs, among them 'Angel of the Resurrection' and 'St. John the Baptist'; the first in pen, the latter in crayon. If we assume they were drawn to test the efficiency of the new process, they have a remarkable force and life. In that same year lithographs were made by William Delamotte, John Claude Nares and Thomas Hearn—each was a painter making tentative experiments. In 1802 many more lithographs were printed by Philipp André. Richard Cooper made the first of his rather sombre crayoned landscapes; R. L. West, son of Benjamin, produced 'Study of a Tree', a beautiful drawing; Richard Corbould and Charles Heath also made lithographs for André; Charles Heath was an engraver of some distinction and his lithographs closely followed the style of his engraving with an excess of pen strokes. Lithography attracted talented amateurs too; throughout the century distinguished, even royal, amateur artists produced lithographs.

Perhaps the first lithographs to be printed which did not appear to be experiments were drawn by the Swiss artist Henry Fuseli. In 1802 he drew with a pen 'A Woman Sitting by the Window', and in 1804 his crayon lithograph, 'The Rape of Ganymed', was printed. Both have life and movement; the crayon drawing is particularly fine. Later Fuseli attempted to illustrate Milton's poetry but, pleasing as were the drawings, the artist achieved little of the poet's inner meaning.

One of the early lithographers I find particularly pleasing is Joseph Fischer. In 1803 he produced 'Tea Table', a charming study of five figures evocative of Jane Austen characters.

Joseph Fischer. Tea Table. 1803. Lithograph

In 1803 André published two series of six prints of pen drawings which he called 'Specimens of Polyautography' and also, together with the publisher Ackermann, 'Twelve Views of Scotland' by Miss F. Waring; one of these views, a rather feeble drawing of Dunkeld Cathedral, can be seen in the British Museum.

By this time, Senefelder and two other André brothers were promoting an interest in lithography in Germany and in 1805 Philipp André left London to join them, handing over the London establishment to G. J. Vollweiler, who left for Europe in 1807. Each had found the demand and interest in London disheartening and financially unrewarding.

There are five crayon drawings of rather classical figures crayoned on to brown paper in the British Museum with the Vollweiler imprint, dated 1807. William Blake's 'Job in Prosperity' was printed as a lithograph while Vollweiler was in London, but it was never published. Sir Geoffrey Keynes in his 'Engravings by W. Blake, the Separate Plates' has said that this Blake lithograph depicts Enoch not Job; possibly Blake found some mystical association between the two.

One of the first attempts to use lithography in book production was made by Thomas Fisher, a clerk in the India Office and an etcher of some skill. He began to prepare a set of books of full-page illustrations of some fresco paintings he claimed to have discovered in a Chapel in Stratford-upon-Avon in 1804. Vollweiler printed fifteen of these lithographs, which were coloured by hand, but after publication of the first part Vollweiler closed down the press in London and returned to Germany. After considerable delay the illustrations were completed with etchings. Not surprisingly, Fisher was incensed by the abrupt cessation of lithography printing in London and wrote bitterly in a letter published in the 'Gentleman's Magazine' of March 1808.

John Thomas Smith's 'Antiquities of Westminster', dated 9th June 1807 on its title page, includes illustrations printed by every known method and can claim to be the first book to contain lithographs with a text.

In 1810, P. S. Munn published a sketchbook of drawings and lessons; unartistic, it is of technical interest only. The first book on lithography to be written in English was published in 1813, as was Thomas Barker's 'Rustic Figures' which contained forty undistinguished drawings printed by Redman, who reopened the press in London after Vollweiler had left.

In Vienna, Senefelder concerned himself with technical improvements, experimenting with calico printing and the substitution of stone by metal plates. He continued to instruct expertly, and English artists were beginning to regret having made so little of their advantage when Senefelder first brought his discovery to London.

Both André and Vollweiler achieved influence and interest in Europe; Redman, who took over in London, achieved little. Until 1818, when Ackermann and Hullmandel began to establish successful lithography publication in London, the initiative had moved to France and Germany. The first attempts in Germany and Austria had been clumsy but, under the guidance of Senefelder, artists such as Strixner, Piloty and Snyder soon perfected a technique which produced superb lithographs.

In France in 1815, two printers, the Comte de Lasteyrie and Englemann, began to popularise the lithograph. At first timid attempts at portraiture and country scenes, often including horses, were made, and laborious execution produced a strange effect, as if they had been traced without the force of direct impact. The first firmly drawn lithograph seems to have been 'Desert Arab' in 1817 by Jean Antoine Gros; hardly a great work of art, it has a technique which prefaces the style of Géricault. In 1818 Englemann published an edition of 'Fables' of La Fontaine, illustrated by pale lithographs made by the Vernet brothers.

If early English lithographers imitated the style of engraving and etching, French artists tended to produce lithographs which resembled paintings; certainly those of Ingres did, especially his 'Reclining Odalisque' of 1825. However, much of the suspicion of the print from stone gave way to an appreciation of the delights and independence of this new language. It required an exceptional graphic artist to display the potential of lithography, and such an artist was Nicolas-Toussaint Charlet, who attained superb effects with crayon, providing unbelievably beautiful tones of velvet and a remarkable range of tone, especially in darker shades. Often his drawings included elements of mist, wind and fire, superbly achieved. Delacroix likened Charlet to Molière and La Fontaine in his sense of drama and vitality. Napoleonic reminiscences abounded in the work of Charlet, as they did in that of his contemporaries Raffet, Vernet, Marlet and Bellanger. Uniforms and battles were depicted with splendid sentimentality; France was in the mood for post-Revolution themes and the woodcut and the etching were considered too slow, too costly; it was a time of preface to the caricature, first political and later social, and lithography satisfied the need for rapidly produced propaganda.

In Germany Englemann was training printers from all over Europe and from his press came lithographs indiscriminately printed for any artists, many of them with indifferent talents. Of the German artists producing lithographs during the nineteenth century, Adolph von Menzel was the most outstanding. His hand-coloured lithographs for 'Uniforms of the Army of Frederick the Great', published between 1851 and 1857, were full of humour with a keen eye for the dignities and absurdities of the militia. In Spain, Francisco de Goya was experimenting with stone and in 1819 he produced

*Adolph von Menzel.
Soldier Bending, from 'The
Army of Frederick the
Great'. 1857. Lithograph*

several deceptively simple lithographs, among them Spanish scenes, 'Sleep', 'Woman Reading Aloud' and 'Force of Love'. In 1825 he drew perhaps the first masterpieces on stone, depicting scenes from the bullfight arena. Goya covered the stone with an even grey ground, then propped it up on an easel as if it were a canvas. He drew with a blunt crayon using a scraper to highlight. By this time his eyesight had deteriorated so that he had to work with a magnifying glass, yet his work is gay, spontaneous and youthful.

It is difficult to disassociate the use of lithography in book illustration from its development in published prints and periodicals. As printers made progress with techniques, more artists were tempted to experiment. In England the development of commercial colour lithography caused artists of originality and quality to ignore the process entirely, but in France such a feeling of debasement was not associated with lithography and the finest artists throughout the century made very beautiful lithographs from time to time, mainly for periodical publication and prints. The new bourgeoisie in France demanded prints for their walls and many reputable artists were grateful for a steady income from this source.

At this time, the Inspector General of Fine Arts and Museums of France was Baron Taylor. His scholarly, academic publication of twenty-four huge folio volumes, containing thousands of illustrations, among them 2,700 lithographs, published between 1820 and 1878 under the title 'Voyages pittoresques et romantiques dans l'Ancienne France' did much to maintain approval and high regard for lithography. In the traditional English topographical books, with the usual tenuous connection between superb illustration and inadequate text, the finest lithographs included were contributed by Fragonard, Bonington, Boys and Isabey.

'Roman Butchers' and 'Standard Bearer' were the first etched-like lithographs by Théodore Géricault, one of the finest original early lithographers in France. After these first uncertain attempts Géricault drew one hundred lithographs during five years. Many of his subjects were horses; at first his creatures were classical Romantic ones, noble with flowing manes. As his technique improved, his horse became a stable creature; Géricault himself said he had abandoned Parnassus for the stable. In 1821, Hullmandel in London printed twelve superb drawings of Géricault, eight of them of horses. The finest of these, 'Entrance to the Adelphi Wharf', is a drawing of three working horses, accompanied by two workmen, so realistic and complete that it evokes a smell of London. Another superb lithograph in the collection, 'Pity the Sorrows of an Old Man', shows the sympathetic skill of Géricault. He had a unique ability to convey atmosphere to the environment and a sense of the comic which he used with great effect from time to time. As early as 1812 Géricault experimented with a second stone to add tint to his lithograph 'Retreat from Moscow'.

Eugène Delacroix wrote in his 'Journal' how he bought an early Géricault lithograph and became inspired immediately by its possibilities. In 1825 Delacroix made a technically remarkable lithograph, 'Macbeth consulting the Witches', using a scraper over the whole design to give the effect of mezzotint. In 1828 he produced an outstanding set of illustrations for Goethe's 'Faust', perhaps the finest book illustrations of all time. Goethe thought Delacroix had found in 'Faust' 'his proper nourishment'. It was an all-too-rare mutual appreciation between author and artist. Also in 1828, Delacroix made several beautiful studies of tigers, relaxed, exotic and original,

Théodore Géricault.
The Return from Russia. 1818.
Lithograph

splendidly sited, using aquatint and pen to provide variety. Later he deserted book illustration for large decorative pieces, but not before he had established himself as one of the great artists in the history of book illustration.

At the same time Henri Monnier was producing fashionable chronicles of everyday scenes. In 1828 he provided some hand-coloured lithographs for Beranger's 'Chanson'; Devéria produced several wood engravings for the same publication. Eugene Lami was making pen drawings of fêtes, balls, races and military occasions; together Monnier and Lami published in 1829–1830 'Voyage en Angleterre', a series of skilfully hand-coloured but monotonous lithographs.

A year earlier, in 1828, Monnier had collaborated with Parkes Bonington to provide lithographs for 'Les Contes du Guy Scaron'. Bonington produced rather tempestuous

Eugène Delacroix. Portrait of Baron Schwiter. 1826. Lithograph

landscapes, not unlike in feeling that evoked by Turner. Several of his delicately drawn lithographs were included in Baron Taylor's 'Voyages pittoresques . . .', mostly of scenes of Normandy and Franche-comte. 'The Clock Tower', dated 1825, is a typical composition with a pleasing combination of architectural accuracy and characterisation by people, horses, dogs. 'Restes et fragments d'architecture du moyen age' contained some of his work, too. It seems impossible to disassociate lithographs by Bonington from those of Thomas Shotter Boys. Several water colours attributed to Bonington may have been painted by Boys, so similar is their choice of subject and atmosphere. To me, Boys appears to have a style more bland, smoother than that of Bonington. To colour lithography Boys brought a high technical skill. It was Boys who made both etchings and colour lithographs for the first volume of Ruskin's 'Stones of Venice', published in 1851. Jean Adhémar has said that through the lithographs of Boys the French came to appreciate their architectural splendours, that Boys did for Paris what Piranesi had done for Rome. The Baron Taylor 'Voyages pittoresques . . .' contained work by Boys, too; he drew scenes from almost every European country and illustrated many travel books. Perhaps his colour lithographs of Paris are the most splendid; the colours are the brightest he achieved. Eventually his colour lithographs were bound into volumes; the most outstanding was 'Picturesque Architecture in Paris, Ghent, Antwerp, Rouen etc.', which was an immediate success both in France and England. The printer Hullmandel considered he had received too little credit for the publication and fascinating correspondence between artists and printer was published in the 'Probe' of 1840.

In 1842, Boys published 'Original Views of London as It Is', containing twenty-seven lithographs produced by drawing lines with a lithographic crayon and adding a beige tint with a second stone, much as Géricault had done thirty years earlier. The colours were added later by hand. Perhaps it is our familiarity with the subject that makes them such a joy to behold; their detail and architectural accuracy show views hardly changed today. Only the carriages, clothing, method of fixing scaffolding, delivering laundry, the design of street lamps seem to have changed, and in 'The Club Houses etc. Pall Mall' even these dated symbols hardly obstruct the feeling of London as it is today.

A bibliography of the work of Boys lists forty-three works from the 'Botanical Cabinet', including plates etched by Boys from 1817 to 1856, the publication date of volume 4 of John Ruskin's 'Modern Painters', which contained two plates etched by Boys after Ruskin. Boys' etching and his signature have an unfinished effect and too

Thomas Shotter Boys. The Strand. 1842. Lithograph

little variation in light, but his lithographs are superb, and postcard reproductions of them remain best-sellers today.

One of the most successful illustrators to contribute to Baron Taylor's 'Voyages Pittoresques . . .' was Jean-Baptiste Isabey. From an early frustrated ambition to be a sailor, Isabey later depicted harbour scenes and estuaries, and his pupil Jongkind continued this theme. Isabey produced mezzotints and six engravings he called 'Souvenirs', perhaps with greater skill than his lithographs, which were often too busily drawn. One lithograph, 'The Return to Harbour', is fine with a powerful excitement which surpasses his other lithographic work.

Paul Huet was another artist attracted to seascapes but his best known lithographs, made in 1829, are small, delicate landscape views of Versailles and Saint-Cloud. He had a feeling for the mystery of trees, and often a detailed foreground would fade beyond in a unique and pleasing manner.

Between 1835 and 1839 Jules Dupré drew many lithographs for 'Artiste', filled with light and space, a preface to the style of Corot, Daubigny and Rousseau. He liked country scenes, rivers, windmills, both in English and French settings. To me his trees are disconcerting, sponge-like and top-heavy, but his compositions are pleasing enough.

At this time in England, a number of exquisite books with hand-coloured lithographs were published in limited editions, now collectors' pieces and extremely valuable. One of the most absorbing of these is Thomas Harral's 'Picturesque View of the Severn', with fifty-two hand-coloured lithographs after the drawings of Samuel Ireland, which describes in considerable detail the towns, castles and natural features of the valley of the Severn. The plates have been printed on paper which is tinted up to the edge of the lithograph and in a few instances the tint has been spread all over the paper and used as a background colouring for the picture.

Some of the finest bird pictures ever published were made by John Gould, one of the outstanding ornithologists of all time. Between 1832 and 1873 he and his collaborators, among them Edward Lear, whom Sacheverell Sitwell has called 'perhaps the best of all bird-painters', produced a total of 2,025 hand-coloured lithographs, which were originally published in parts in cloth boxes and later bound into the finest books ever produced. 'The Birds of Europe' was issued in 22 parts and later in 5 volumes in 1837; between 1850 and 1883 'The Birds of Asia' in 35 parts, forming 7 volumes; 'A Monograph of the Trochilidae, or Family of Humming Birds', between 1849 and 1887 in 25 parts and later 5 volumes; and 'The Birds of Great Britain', in 25 parts bound into 5 volumes between 1862 and 1873. With R. B. Sharpe, John Gould produced 'The Birds of New Guinea and the Adjacent Papuan Islands', in 25 parts and 5 volumes, between 1875 and 1888. Together these books comprise one of the most magnificent collections ever produced.

Grandville. Advertisement for 'La Caricature'. 1830. Lithograph

In terms of the commercial development of lithography, a most important event was the first issue in Paris on the 4th of November 1830 of the weekly 'La Caricature'. Edited by Charles Philippon, it was first announced as a 'moral, religious, theatrical publication'. It ran for 250 issues; by its 100th edition it had added 'political' to its title. Obviously on such publications caricaturists must thrive, and from the beginning Philippon employed artists such as Charles, Pigal, Huet, Monnier and Grandville. In 1832 the first lithograph appeared by Honoré Daumier, and from that time the wit, humour and savagery of the art of Daumier made 'La Caricature' a weapon of concern to the Establishment. For the first time, it seems, an artist found that for superb direct effect from a drawing on stone, the minimum of strokes was required. In this way Daumier achieved more obvious attitudes, immediate impact, and from his first contribution he achieved extremes of the sublime and the grotesque. Philippon brought out another weekly, 'Le Charivari', in 1832 and Daumier produced enormous quantities of drawings for both publications. 'Le Charivari' had a pleasure-seeking but moral tone, and for it Daumier used his uncanny art to gauge the contemporary scene. Injustices he made household discontents; officials were brilliantly and often brutally caricatured. He measured the Republican mood of France better than any other artist, and he led the *bourgeoisie* to demand standards they might never have expressed themselves. There was little grace about his work, yet in the drawing of a

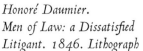
Honoré Daumier.
Men of Law: a Dissatisfied
Litigant. 1846. Lithograph

finger so much expression. Perhaps his best known drawing is that superbly smug 'Men of Law—a Dissatisfied Litigant', the man of law looking remarkably like the early TV Dr. Who and the litigant so brilliantly contemptuous.

Through Daumier, Charles Philippon expressed his militant liberalism and eventually Daumier was imprisoned for six months for his disrespect towards the sovereign and political commentary was censored; on his release, he turned to social satire and later to more serious studies.

Daumier used 'old bits of crayon' that other artists would have discarded but, by so doing, he discovered original strokes. Often he touched up his work with pen or brushes, yet his pen drawing was undistinguished. He applied liquid ink on to stone with a small brush and a broken tooth-comb, a method favoured later by poster artists. Mostly he used a subtle range of greys, with liberal use of the scraper.

Daumier described his talent as 'no heroics, no ideal figures, I am of my own time', yet Baudelaire doubted that anyone possessed a greater sense of grandeur or of classical times than Daumier. His later work had an epic quality. He made a long series of plates on European questions, employing symbols of antiquity, cannon, eagles, Mars, Time with sickle, tombstones. 'France' he depicted as a tree blasted by lightning, accompanied by the words 'Luckily the roots are deep'. 'Peace' shows Death in a straw hat, astride a rock, playing a trumpet, and 'Freedom' depicts the Constitution trying on a dress.

Daumier illustrated only one book, 'Les Cent et un Robert-Macaire', providing caricatures rather than illustrations to accompany an unusually substantial text by Alhoy Huart. Daumier relied much upon his own imagination and must have found a text restricting to his art. Four thousand lithographs published between 1829 and 1872 are attributed to Daumier; it is no exaggeration to say that through them he expressed the soul of France.

It is difficult to assess the influence of Daumier on his contemporary artists; certainly it was considerable. Paul Gavarni was encouraged by Daumier to lessen the severity of his work and to eliminate excessive detail. Gavarni's life was that of a fashionable dandy—he flitted from scene to scene, rarely remaining long enough to develop sympathies. Nevertheless he drew fabrics supremely well—velvets, silks, tweeds—and the portrait which he drew in 1853 of 'The Brothers Goncourt' is fine if somewhat melancholy.

Another portrait artist of quality was Achille Devéria. His nudes had less style than those of Ingres, but he had great skill in portraying rather young, voluptuous girls with a tenderness and softness, often in a sunny or moonlit environment. More serious portrait studies included Victor Hugo, Dumas, de Vigny, Liszt, Lemercier and Lamartine. All were vividly alive, without flourish or excess of detail.

The Swiss, Rodolphe Töpffer, was often likened to Rowlandson as he made many comic lithographs, but his native feeling for mountains was rather special. 'Landscape with Folly' is a fine example of the feeling of air and height he achieved—a technique not unlike some of Turner's dry-point and aquatint work in 'Liber Studiorum'.

Achille Devéria.
Portrait of Victor Hugo.
1829. Lithograph

The printing of lithography declined in the middle of the nineteenth century, perhaps as a reaction to the enormous bulk of colour or chromo-lithography produced in England at that time. In France there was a revival of the lithograph towards the end of the century, less in book illustration than in the form of single prints. Many of the periodicals issued prints from time to time, charging an extra franc or so for such a supplement. 'The Sower' by Jean-François Millet reached many thousands of French homes in this way and remains today one of the best-known nineteenth-century lithographs.

Edouard Manet made twenty-one lithographs and a great many more etchings. 'The Balloon', his first lithograph, 'The Barricade' dated 1871 and several on Civil War themes show clearly the influence of Daumier, as did his several portraits. However, perhaps his best known lithograph is the very original 'The Races'. Almost a cursory scribbling technique manages to convey speed in a remarkable manner. Manet was influenced, too, by the work of Japanese artists, as is shown in his illustrations for Edgar Allan Poe's poem 'The Raven'. In black and white, they are vigorous and imaginative with a paint-like quality and it may be said that Manet was the first painter since Delacroix to work at the lithograph process with success. Doré made some over-sentimental wood-engravings for the same poem some eight years later; by comparison the Manet illustrations are superbly uncomplicated.

If Manet was affected by the art of Daumier and the Japanese, he himself influenced later artists including Toulouse-Lautrec. In 1874 Manet made a colour lithograph 'Punchinello', using seven stones to achieve great variety of colour tone, and this drawing of a somewhat comic fictional military figure aroused great interest. Twenty years later Toulouse-Lautrec produced rather similar figures with little background interest but with superb colour tone.

One contemporary and friend of Daumier who owes nothing to his influence was Camille Corot. The charm of his lithographs is in their composition, complete from

Camille Corot. Reminiscences of Italy. 1871. Lithograph

conception, drawn partly from memory and partly from sketches. He never made additions, alterations or made use of the scraper. In 1871 he produced twelve 'autographies', pleasing compositions with that total inter-relationship between parts so characteristic of his work. His method of outlining trees gives them movement as if seen from a passing train. His drawing was tenuous, unsubstantial, often peppered with humble inhabitants. One of the most charming of Corot's lithographs 'The Church Tower of St. Nicolas-les-Arras' he drew in 1870, so expressive of the countryside of France. Corot made many Italian landscapes too, unmistakably of their region, drawn with the same deceptively simple technique.

Edgar Degas made his first lithograph in 1875, but like Corot, book illustration does not seem to have attracted him at any time. In his early life as an artist Degas had a meticulous style; later he produced work with much alteration. One of his lithographs, 'After the Bath', shows correction to an extraordinary degree, but many of his lithographs were very beautiful. One delightful one, 'Madame Bécat aux Ambassadeurs', has superb effects of chandelier light and welcoming warmth.

Fantin-Latour experimented rather unsuccessfully with lithography although he did produce illustrations for a book on Wagner in 1886 and for another on Berlioz in 1888. His work was rather colourless, with pallid, sexless people with little sense of movement. Fantin-Latour is an obvious example of the dangers lithography can hold for even the most competent painters.

Odilon Redon, one of the most imaginative and certainly the most disconcerting French artist since Delacroix, who with strange macabre forms explored the unknown world, made marvellously dramatic use of black and white, particularly when he wished to convey extremes of heat or light. What superb book illustrations he might have made!

With the obvious exception of Daumier, Toulouse-Lautrec had the greatest lithographic output in France during the nineteenth century. From 1892 to 1900 he produced more than 400 lithographs, including 50 in colour and 10 which he drew for 'Elles'. Toulouse-Lautrec showed an extraordinary sense of delight in earthly, ordinary things. Bonnard had introduced him to lithography and in 1892 he began as a poster artist; soon his rather angular shapes were to be seen everywhere. Around the same time Aubrey Beardsley was experimenting with lithography for display posters in London. There is something of Hokusai's ink drawings, of Manet, and Whistler, too, in the work of Toulouse-Lautrec, and in spite of his short, embittered personal life he made rather special relationships with fellow artists and authors. In 1898 he

Henri de Toulouse-Lautrec. Lithographs

123

produced enchanting lithographic illustrations for 'Au Pied du Surai' by Clemenceau; the cynicism of Clemenceau suited him to perfection. A year later he illustrated Jules Renard's 'Histoires Naturelles', exploiting humour from the world of animals with extraordinary skill. No artist since Fragonard had combined poetry, vision and eroticism with such apparent simplicity.

By the end of the century, few of the great artists in France ignored lithography completely. Renoir produced many seemingly hasty compositions with that unique charm and sensitivity apparent in all of his work. Eugène Carrière drew several fine portraits, their faces emerging from soft backgrounds; Paul Gauguin produced lithographs of his Tahiti friends, which were printed on yellow paper and published in 'L'Estampe Originale'; and Rodin made several lithographs in his water-colour style, among them illustrations for 'Jardin des Supplices'. One Rodin lithograph, 'New Idol', is superb, depicting two forms emerging from a blend of light and shade, very like in effect that achieved by Carrière.

The American, James McNeill Whistler, made a great many lithographs of Paris and London scenes, almost all of them drawn on transfer paper with that strange rubbed-out effect; many are strongly crayoned, but more often they are drawn to suggest rather than to describe with a lightness of touch especially pleasing in his drawings of young girls and nudes; many of these drawings appeared in Roger-Marx's 'L'Estampe Originale'.

Bonnard first made use of lithography in his poster work and his enthusiasm had persuaded Toulouse-Lautrec to do likewise. Bonnard had a marked fondness for those colours associated with Japanese prints, greens, reds and neutral colours—and his figures had a strange flatness. Often he left broken outlines for the imagination to complete; certainly his compositions had great originality and contributed to the enthusiasm of A. S. Hartwick, who had worked with Bonnard in Paris; Hartwick founded the Senefelder Club in 1900 in London, introducing the artist print to England.

Forain, who made his first lithograph in 1890, produced many detailed social studies of manners and behaviour. His men were top-hatted and moustached, his women hunted creatures. Most of his scenes were furtive, theatrical, menacing, depicting poverty and monotony. With the same material Toulouse-Lautrec would have found prettiness and delight, but the ill-humour of Forain thundered their atmosphere.

Edouard Vuillard produced slightly oppressive, busy lithographs, less skilful than his painting; and Maurice Denis made a number of domestic studies quite unlike his later work. Denis illustrated in 1893 André Gide's 'Voyage d'Urien', before he deserted lithography for wood engraving. Pissaro made sixty-seven lithographs, many of them of lively Paris scenes, but he considered his impressionist lithographs inferior to his etching; and in 1898 Cézanne made his well-known colour lithograph 'Bathers', a pleasing composition of pattern and subdued colour.

Every artist of talent seems to have experimented with lithography, but most considered it a means of easily reproducing work for periodical publication. Perhaps the years of Daumier's success had reduced the lithograph to association with the comic cartoon. Certainly with the coming of photography the commercial lithograph coarsened in production, minimising the one undisputed advantage over other forms of illustration, that of direct artist control. What seems extraordinary is that commercial colour lithography produced in such bulk from 1840 in England should have remained so insular, more especially as it was Engelmann in Paris who patented in 1837 full colour-printed lithography, which he called 'chromolithography'. Hullmandel in London, who printed a great deal of fine-quality work, including Boys' 'Picturesque Architecture' in 1839, himself patented a process in 1840 which he called 'lithotint' where colours were added to highlight a print in black and neutral tones. Early lithotints in the 1840's were imitations of wash drawings on tinted paper subsequently coloured by hand. By comparison with the chromolithographs, they are delicate and very light and pleasing, if rather unoriginal. Even the added colour was usually rather muted in tone and the large numbers of prints published became favourite drawing-room adornments. Many of them were issued, as in France, supplementary to popular journals of the day and subsequently bound into volumes. Not surprisingly, they now seem rather faded and monotonous, without impact. Many of these early lithotints were published by Charles Tilt; in 1836 he published J. D. Harding's 'Sketches at Home and Abroad', adding a neutral tone to black and subsequently adding soft greens and blues. His 'Pearls of the East', published in 1837, included twelve lithographs, two of them coloured, and he published, too, a series of large art books over a number of years to which George Cruikshank contributed from time to time. The Tilt publications were printed by Hullmandel, who with Ackermann was one of the first two publishers to produce lithography of any quality in London. Hullmandel printed in 1839 T. S. Boys' 'Picturesque Architecture . . .' which, although wholly printed with four colours in addition to black, avoided the garish quality of fully printed chromolithography.

The vast tomes of coloured plates published from the 1840's could not have been printed earlier by any other method, which explains their great number and popularity. So often the size of the volume reduced the artistic impact even in those more tastefully produced, such as in David Roberts' 'The Holy Land, Syria, Idumea, Arabia, Egypt and Nubia' which contained one hundred and twenty-four plates, at first published in parts from 1842–5 and later in three volumes, the last dated 1849. Ruskin wrote in 'Praeterita', 'they were faithful and laborious beyond any outlines from nature I had ever seen'. Drawn on the spot, they measured 24 inches × 17 inches; perhaps before photography such work had great appeal, yet Ruskin also called them 'a kind of grey mirror'. 'Laborious' and 'grey' they seem certainly today.

In 1834, a young Welsh architect, Owen Jones, visited Spain, where he became fascinated by the Alhambra Palace. With the French architect Jules Goury, who died of cholera during the trip, Jones made drawings of the Palace with extraordinary precision. On his return to England, Owen Jones aimed to reproduce the drawings in flat bright colours to be formed into a geometrical pattern. He set up his own press near Charing Cross and from there between 1836 and 1841 the first volume of 'Alhambra' was published in ten parts, and the second volume in two parts, measuring $25\frac{5}{8}$ inches × $19\frac{1}{4}$ inches; the illustrations included woodcuts by Henry Vizetelly, one hundred and four copper and steel engravings, mainly of plans, elevations and views, a few zinc lithographs and sixty-nine chromolithographs printed in six or seven colours with much gold embossing. The immediate impact is one of disbelief. This massive work has such vigorous colouring that it appears crude and unartistic, although volume two shows an improvement in Jones's technique. Priced at £36 10s. it was hardly a popular success, yet 'Alhambra' was the forerunner of a great new industry which was to become one of the most characteristic of the early Victorian age. The 'chromolithographed illuminated gift book', as it became known, with themes of history, art, the Church and naturalism, became the ideal symbol of the Victorian Sunday. Kenneth Clark has said that the fashion for illumination may be considered part of the Gothic Revival both in its early suitability for Sunday occupation and, later in the nineteenth century, as a subject for serious study and pleasure. Certainly the introduction of chromolithography provided a great aid to the study of art, if more visual than historical.

Between 1841 and 1851 Owen Jones illuminated at least fifteen books, the first published by Murray, a lavish edition of J. G. Lockhart's 'Ancient Spanish Ballads'. Jones contributed four chromolithographs, borders, decorative initials and vignettes, but the book was illustrated mainly with wood engravings and every page had lavish woodcut borders in red, yellow, green and grey. A certain disharmony exists between the styles of the woodcut and the chromo-lithograph and the book is more of interest than of beauty.

In 1842 Owen Jones made ten chromolithographs for 'Designs for Mosaic and Tesellated Pavements'; in 1843 he made three more for Henry Gally Knight's 'Ecclesiastical Architecture of Italy'; and in 1844 several for the second volume of Weale's 'Quarterly Papers on Architecture'. He contributed to several more until 1851 and then he became involved with his major work, 'The Grammar of Ornament', published in 1856. By any standards this is a superb picture book with one hundred and fourteen pages of text expounding his theories on ornament and a vast number of plates drawn on stone by Francis Bedford. The variety of scales and styles, and an appreciation of texture quite beyond the scope of the camera, combine to make it an exciting work.

Many later books have Owen Jones's illuminations too, among them Thomas Moore's 'Paradise and the Peri' in 1860, with Henry and Albert Warren, who collaborated with Jones again in 1865 in 'Joseph and His Brethren' and in 1866 for 'Scenes from the Winter's Tales', using between six and seven colours in most, and as many as thirteen in a few of the illustrations. In 1861–2 Jones produced what he considered his masterpiece, 'The Victorian Psalter', an illuminated edition of the Psalms. The printed version is rather gloomy with a rigid monotony of reds, blues and golds, although in the Jones's original drawings at the Victoria and Albert Museum the blues are much more vibrant. Jones was beginning to make tortuous designs with his lettering; often initial letters were only comprehensible because they linked with the following part of the word. All of his later work suffers from painful lettering design including Tennyson's poem 'A Welcome to Alexandra' and 'The Wedding at Windsor', both published in 1863, and both of them gay and colourful, as was his 'Sunday Book'. He seemed obsessed by the potential extremes of the designs of letters and in 1864 he published '1,001 Initial letters' and later the same year '702 Monograms'.

In France, the earliest use of the lithotint was in 1832 by Count Bastard for his 'Peintures et Manuscrits', an enormous volume of magnificently coloured illustrations. Chromolithography was used in Germany as early as 1828 by Zahn and by Boetticher in 1832–42. In 1841 the mammoth four-volumed folio work of Silvestre, 'Paléographie Universelle', was published in Paris, a remarkable work including paleography from Mexico, Peru and all of the main European countries. Illustrations included both lithotints and chromolithographs, the best of which are superior to those in Owen Jones's 'Alhambra'. Silvestre's great work was later reprinted in London by Hanhart.

But chromolithography was essentially a Victorian art, ostentatious in the most impressive manner. It was a time for the designer with an eye for over-embellishment, and if it horrified the sensitivity of artists, it gladdened the lives of the Victorian public.

Henry Shaw, essentially a scholar and antiquarian, attempted to portray historical accuracies; Owen Jones, a truly superb draughtsman, concerned himself largely with fashionable embellishment of an architectural past; and a prolific contemporary, Noel Humphreys, endeavoured to revitalise and re-create a feeling of the Italian art he found so magical. Jones and Humphreys collaborated to produce a folio of coloured manuscripts in 1844 which they called 'Illuminated Books of the Middle Ages' and in 1849 Noel Humphreys produced an exquisite small handbook for students wishing to practise art, 'The Art of Illumination'. He used fourteen colours in his twelve chromolithographs and designed a very pretty white leather binding for it. Not since Blake had such regard for decoration been seen as that by Humphreys. His years in Italy had left an impression often seen in his work; much of it had greater power and originality than anything produced by Owen Jones. His 'Coins of England', published by William Smith in 1846, is delightful; it became immediately so popular that by 1849 a sixth edition had appeared. For it, Humphreys made twenty-four chromo-lithographed plates printed in gold, silver and copper on a royal blue background. The binding he designed to resemble crimson moiré. In 1847 the Vizetelly Brothers published Humphreys' 'Parables of Our Lord'; thirty-two chromolithographs, many showing a love of flowers, were bound into a papier maché binding simulated as carved ebony. Humphreys produced many more books, usually with biblical, artistic, poetic or naturalist themes. One of the most striking was 'A Record of the Black Prince', among the best known gift books of the time, and with unusually black type. Humphreys' books were consistently rich examples of Victorian Gothic design. After 1851 he turned to writing books and to making wood engravings. He produced botanical illustrations and monochrome decoration for several books by other authors and in 1859 he experimented with reasonable success on a two-colour publication of Goldsmith's poems.

Owen Jones and Noel Humphreys set the fashionable pace for many years. Their work was designed consciously in every detail and their influence extended to Christmas cards, music covers and eventually to Walter Crane and the Kelmscott Press of

Aubrey Beardsley. Merlin, from 'Le Morte D'Arthur'. 1893

the 1890's. It is doubtful that William Morris or Aubrey Beardsley would have drawn as they did if the mood had not long been established. Yet in no way could Jones and Humphreys be compared with artists producing original lithographs. Their influence grew from a vision of pattern that could be built with colour lithography and coincided with the Victorian nadir of the arts, when colour itself had greater meaning than art.

9

One of the earliest rivals to Owen Jones was Michael Hanhart, who founded a press in Charlotte Street in the 1830's. The Hanhart company was the first important printer of chromolithographed music covers, but he was responsible for the printing and supervision, too, of several impressive books. Almost richer than Jones' 'Alhambra' was his publication in 1844, Pugin's 'Glossary of Ecclesiastical Ornament and Costume'. A smaller popular edition was published in 1849 called 'Floriated Ornament'. It was Hanhart, too, who printed the English edition of Silvestre's 'Paléographie Universelle'.

During the remainder of the nineteenth century, books with chromolithographs flowed from the printing presses. Many of those which attract today contain illustrations produced by several methods; certainly these present a more restful effect.

Themes were taken from every fashionable aspect of art, from mosaics, from ecclesiastical decoration, in particular stained glass and metal work, but as the century progressed the looking themes gave way slowly to more practical ones and books became smaller and instructive.

In 1846 Edward Lear's 'Book of Nonsense' was published with lithographs, but later editions contained wood engravings of the same design. In 1848 came 'Struwwelpeter', the first of a spate of cheap 'toy books' for children, and thus began another Victorian favourite. Often printed on woolly paper with smudged illustrations with both the design and type unbelievably ugly, they satisfied a need and were bought for every child in the land.

The Great Exhibition, too, provided reason for a spate of chromolithography; by now lithography was commercially cheaper than engraving. Digby Wyatt's 'Industrial Arts of the Nineteenth Century', produced for the 1851 Exhibition, was a remarkable compendium of work by artists from many nations.

By the 1860's the market for chromolithographed books was facing competition from wood engraving, and artists rather than designers were beginning to take a new interest in illustration as an art form. Books cherished at that time by Victorian children had delicately coloured wood engravings neatly printed between the text, and the function of the chromolithograph began to narrow to a rather specialist and more scholarly field.

In the earlier brilliantly illuminated books, almost always the typography faded feebly in competition with the illustration, and any book with a strong well-balanced typography was printed invariably by Whittingham or Pickering. But now scholars who were using chromolithographed books were beginning to have concern for the skill of the typographer. Winckelmann in Berlin and Firmin-Didot at the Imperial Printing Office of Vienna produced magnificent typographic work, and in France Hangard-Mange was endeavouring to attain a standard to 'discourage French artists from taking their work to Vienna and Berlin'. Engelmann and Graf produced a great deal of superbly scholarly work too, and it was to these printers that most of the finest work produced in England was taken. London publishers, a few of whom remain today, were setting up houses in considerable numbers. If the size and splendour of publications had diminished, the demand certainly had not. 1857 had seen the first book published where photographs were transferred to lithographic stones, J. Pouncy's 'Dorsetshire Photographically Illustrated', but it was many years before this became commercially economic. Meanwhile smaller, even pocket books of poems, Shakespeare, and Victorian novels were appearing, many of them illustrated, though few by lithography. But books of instruction published on newly exciting possibilities, which were a Victorian forerunner of a series such as 'Teach Yourself', and a large number of natural history books of observation often did have lithographs as illustrations. Joseph Cundall contributed a considerable sense of moderate taste to Victorian design in the latter half of the nineteenth century and persuaded artists such as John Gilbert, better known as a wood engraver, to make chromolithographs to illustrate the works of Shakespeare; and two Liverpool architects, W. and G. Audsley, produced agreeable books on floral decoration and instruction books on every domestic interest.

Perhaps the Victorian book-buying public after the publication of so many gentle wood engravings during the 1860's, tired of the gawdy, bulky books so often associated with chromolithography. England had seen so little original lithography and the tastelessness of most chromolithography must have actively discouraged any sensitive artist to use this medium.

The lithograph fitted the mood of Victorian activity as no other illustrative method could have done. How much less exciting would have been nineteenth-century publishing if it had not been invented.

Bibliography

ADHÉMAR, Jean. Graphic art of the eighteenth century. Thames & Hudson, 1964.

BEWICK, Thomas. A Memoir. 1822–1828.

BINYON, Laurence. The followers of William Blake. Halton & Truscott Smith, 1925.

BLAND, David. A history of book illustration; the illuminated manuscript and the printed book. Faber, 1958.

BLAND, David. The illustration of books. 3rd edition. Faber, 1962.

BLISS, Douglas Percy. A history of wood engraving. Dent, 1928.

BRUNNER, Felix. A handbook of graphic reproduction processes. Tiranti, 1962.

CARTER, J. *and* CRUTCHLEY, B. The printed book. 3rd edition. Cambridge University Press, 1951.

CLARK, *Lord*

    The Gothic Revival. Constable, 1928.

    Landscape into art. Murray, 1949.

    Moments of vision. Romanes Lecture. 1954.

    Ruskin today. Murray, 1964.

CORFIATO, Hector, *editor*. Piranesi compositions. Tiranti, 1962.

GRAPHIS. 1948 to date.

HERKOMER, Sir Hubert von. The Slade Lectures, Oxford. Macmillan, 1892.

HILLIER, J. Japanese masters of the colour print. 2nd edition. Phaidon Press, 1954.

HOLME, Geoffrey, *editor*. British book illustration yesterday and today, with a commentary by Malcolm C. Salaman. Studio, 1923.

IRVINS, William M. Prints and visual communication. Routledge, 1953.

LAMB, Lynton. Drawing for illustration. Oxford University Press, 1962.

LINTON, W. J. The Masters of wood engraving. 1889.

McLEAN, Ruari.

    The Reminiscences of Edmund Evans. Oxford, Clarendon Press, 1967.

    Victorian book design and colour printing. Faber, 1963.

MAHONEY, Bertha *and others*. Illustrators of children's books, 1744–1945. Horn Books Incorporated, 1947.

MALRAUX, André. Saturn; an essay on Goya. Phaidon Press, 1957.

MORISON, Stanley. Four centuries of fine printing. Ernest Benn, 1924.

OTTLEY, H. A biographical and critical dictionary of recent and living painters and engravers. 1886.

PAPILLON, J. M. Traité historique et pratique de la gravure en bois. 3 volumes. Paris, 1776.

BIBLIOGRAPHY

Penell, J. Lithography and lithographers, 1915.

Pollard, A. W. Fine books. London, 1912.

Rayner, John. A selection of engravings on wood by Thomas Bewick. Penguin, 1947.

Reid, Forrest. Illustrators of the sixties. Faber, 1928.

Roger-Marx, Claude. Graphic art of the nineteenth century. Thames & Hudson, 1962.

Ruskin, John. Modern painters. 5 volumes. 1873.

Sparrow, Walter Shaw. A book of British etching from Francis Barlow to Francis Seymour Haden. John Lane, 1926.

Stone, Reynolds. Wood engravings of Thomas Bewick reproduced in collotype, selected with a biographical introduction. Hart-Davis, 1953.

White, Gleeson. English illustrations: the sixties. Constable, 1906.

Zigrosser, Carl. The book of fine prints. Owen, 1937.

Index to Names

Italic figures are used to indicate pages containing an illustration

Aubrey Beardsley. Merlin, from 'Le Morte D'Arthur'. 1893